F. GEORGE KAY

The Family in Transition

ITS PAST, PRESENT, AND FUTURE PATTERNS

DAVID & CHARLES
NEWTON ABBOT

ISBN 0 7153 5568 6

Set in 11/13 point Plantin
and printed in Great Britain
by W J Holman Limited Dawlish Devon
for David & Charles (Publishers) Limited
South Devon House   Newton Abbot   Devon

THE
FAMILY
IN TRANSITION

PEOPLE, PLANS AND PROBLEMS SERIES

General editor: Professor J. B. Mays
             Department of Sociology,
             University of Liverpool

published

> *From School to Work*   Kenneth Roberts
> A Study of the Youth Employment Service

in preparation

> *Friends in Need*   Patrick Goldring
> The Story of the Family Service Units
>
> *A New Bill of Rights*   Frank Stacey
>
> *Penal Reform*   Merfyn Turner
>
> *Planning and Human Need*   Philip Heywood
>
> *Pressure Groups*   Bridget Pym
>
> *The Sociology of Race*   Gideon Ben-Tovim
>
> *Violence*   John Gunn

Contents

1 *Sex, Marriage and Family in a Changing Society*

The family, the oldest of human institutions, is also the smallest unit of men and women which has any influence on society and the State. To religionists the family exists through the will of God and must therefore be maintained in an unchanging pattern as set out in whatever dogma a particular belief lays down. To anthropologists it is a natural growth which has been moulded and protected by a series of taboos and conventions which succeeding generations of society have deemed of value until other ideas appear to justify new experiment and a gradual abandonment of older customs.

The evolution of the family has thus been a slow but continuing process of selection, test and occasional rejection in the search for a more suitable structure of unity in a prevailing social culture. If any family pattern ceases to adapt and change according to circumstances it must weaken and ultimately die. Such overall rigidity is unthinkable: the human regard for the family is so fundamental that it has always evolved to meet the needs of its members. The family has never been rejected; it has merely changed in form. There has never been a golden age of family life, and presumably never will be. But there can easily be a dark age, if society and the State attempt to erode the status of the family by demanding that the individual first and foremost be a citizen and subject, and only secondarily a husband, father, and son, or wife, mother, and daughter.

The current widespread criticism and pessimism about the Western family are a symptom of the attempts of society and the State to gain superiority, and a warning of the menace to human happiness. Economic, political and natural influences have moulded the family over millenia into a shape approved by Western society. Any sign of spontaneous change is now at risk of being regarded as dangerous, as indeed it may well be to the established order. Yet, if history has any lesson for contemporary experiment, change will not necessarily be injurious to the family, which has frequently evolved new patterns of living for its own welfare in advance of the attitude of the society of which it was a part.

The Western family pattern now being subjected to well-nigh irresistible forces of economic and scientific evolution developed from cultures of ancient civilisations, modified by Judaic-Christian teachings on marriage. On this foundation the gradual progress of industrialisation in the eighteenth and early nineteenth centuries imposed changes during which the State and Church frequently competed, but more often were in alliance, for the control of the activities and behaviour of members of the family. In the nineteenth and twentieth centuries a two-fold development occurred. The family began to assert its independence, slowly obtaining greater freedom for the principal individuals in it and particularly with more tolerance of the personal desires of the couple who formed its nucleus. Partly as a reaction to this attitude, there developed a greater degree of intervention by the State in the lives of family members, particularly the offspring, ostensibly for the benefit of the individual. These two influences, mutually hostile almost as often as they were mutually advantageous, increased in the twentieth century. The pace of change is now likely to accelerate.

The characteristics of Western marriage were for generation after generation based on permanent monogamy, a patriarchal head, and insistence that junior members shall obey and respect the seniors. All these traits of family were understandably approved by society and the State. All are now being challenged by the family itself, suggesting that old standards may indeed by inimical to its future, and new ones are needed for its survival.

The assumption that the Establishment-approved type of Western family is the only one which is acceptable on grounds of individual happiness, religious law, and social stability means that all other forms, past, present, or future, must be dismissed as destructive, which they were and are not. Nor is the preoccupation with infringements of the traditional sexual code justified as a reason to insinuate that the Western family is already in fragmentation. The breaking of sexual taboos in the family cult has regularly been as prevalent as obedience to sexual conventions. The family has always survived them intact. The real danger to the family is in a growth of the State's interference in family customs and behaviour, usually masquerading as loftily inspired actions designed to benefit the family, but in reality motivated by the State's considerations of its own power and even survival. The family need not worry: it will successfully resist action to enforce undesired and injurious change. Its inviolability lies in the fact that it does not exist solely for economic benefit or even for any practical motive of human reasoning which could be changed by exterior forces. It is fundamentally a state of emotional harmony, irrational and therefore as inexplicable as it is imperishable. The fact that the dynastic importance of the family has declined is merely an example of modern adulation of the present and disregard for the past. It has meant that families are born and die within two or three generations, but are none the less a social force in spite of this ephemeral style.

Mate selection has become almost entirely the independent action of the man and woman concerned. Parents are rarely consulted and not often asked for their approval. Only in families where pressures of money, and to a lesser extent protection or advancement of their social position, can be exerted, is the intention to marry and mate selection affected by parental opinion.. The State shows its approval of a semblance of parental authority by allowing parents to forbid marriage of offspring for a brief period between the minimum legal age for marriage and adult independence. This has been reduced in Britain and some parts of the United States by lowering the age at which parents cease to control their children from twenty-one to eighteen. The State approves of a challenge to parental authority by allowing minors to apply to the courts for permission to marry, and it is for the parents to state a valid objection. Usually this objection can be overcome by the daughter becoming pregnant, an unchallengeable gesture of defiance which the State condones.

About a quarter of all single men and women in Britain between the ages of eighteen and twenty-nine live away from the parental home.[1] When children reach the age of seventeen only difficult and expensive court proceedings can prevent their leaving the family circle. Thus at the age when courtship is natural, at least four million young British people are living unsupervised and independent lives. In addition, the culture of the younger generation ensures that those who remain in the parental home spend most of their working and recreational time with their own generation, with little or no parental control of what they do or whom they meet.

Consequently contacts with potential mates are due largely to haphazard meetings in college, amusement centre, and workplace, where it is improbable that a friendship will be struck up with anyone previously well known to the parents of the couple concerned. It is today more likely that a marriage results from identity of interests in a recreational activity, in office or at factory bench, or through mutual aid in studies. That the majority of these marriages are approved or at least accepted by the parents on both sides, and some measure of unity between the two families then occurs, is a testimonial to the tolerance of the older generation, not of any consideration by the courting couple.

The revolution in attitudes may well strengthen monogamous life of the conventional kind. If people marry solely for emotional considerations, and are not influenced by third parties, one may presume that all those vital but intangible factors which enable two people happily to live together are able to flourish. But the dynastic family must suffer because of this fundamentally selfish and narrow attitude. Each generation, on reaching maturity, launches a new family, weakly connected to the two elder groups from which it has originated. When children arrive the grandparents know that it will be wise not to interfere lest the fragility of the generation links are further weakened by outright disputes.

The modern stress on romantic motives for marriage encourages an underlying fear of making a mistake in selecting a mate with whom to found a family. Young people feel that sexual attraction is not enough (hence their discrimination between a sexual adventure and a legalised union). Courtship becomes a gamble, and there are few experienced advisers on how to win, now that parental opinion is dismissed as biased or out-of-date. Hence the growing popularity of the professional matchmaker. Computers are widely used by young men and women in the higher education group, their faith in the machine's wisdom so great that they gladly supply a welter of intimate details to be fed into the computer bank which they would be chary of revealing to anyone but a psychiatrist.

A more sensitive service is that of the National Marriage Guidance Council in Britain, an organisation approved and financially supported by the State. It has more than 600 counsellors selected and trained for educational work. Their aims are stated to be 'to help young people towards making a realistic and rewarding relationship'. It is noteworthy that the Council's information material for young people explains: 'Marriage is a matter of relationships and the ability to make relationships is not inborn. It is learnt through contact with parents and others. By helping them to think of themselves in relation to others and to society we try to support young people through the turbulent, emotional period of adolescence.'[2] The inference, perhaps rightly, is that prospective clients have not benefited from contact with parents and other older people.

The need many persons feel for the help which their families no longer give is also shown by the enormous increase in the use of marriage organisers. According to the British Council of Churches as many as a thousand marriage bureaux operate in Britain. The six large ones, which cover the whole country and also have overseas clients on their books, average about 25,000 registrations a year. Dating agencies flourish in the USA, some matching their clients by computer. The idea is, of course, very old; a professional expert supporting the belief that marriage should not be left to the emotional impulses of two people but must take into consideration the economic and social benefits of any marriage.

The present era is exceptional in sanctioning disassociation of sexual activity, marriage, and family establishment. Each can exist, and even flourish, by itself, without real hindrance from economic and social pressures. Lovers need not marry and can prevent the birth of children. A couple may wed as the result of personal motives without being in love or, indeed, pledging the abandonment of existing or future sexual liaisons. An unmarried mother, uncertain of the paternity of her child, can become head of a new family. These divergences from the norm are admittedly in a minority and liable to individual censure, but the State tolerates them.

Behaviour patterns, social influences, and traditions still persuade the majority of people to conform to the conventional sequence of courtship, marriage, and family life. Considering the ease with which hedonistic and irresponsible practices of promiscuity and ephemeral partnerships can be adopted it is remarkable that life-long monogamy as the pivot of a family existence remains so widespread a culture, and the desire of the majority, notably the young.

The number of marriages in Britain increased from 291,000 in 1901 to 452,000 in 1968, an increase of 55 per cent in a period when the population grew by 44 per cent.[3] In the United States in 1900 there were 709,000 marriages, and in 1968, 2,069,000, an increase of 191 per cent during a period when the population increased by 160 per cent. The increase is partly due to improved standards of living, for marriage remains something of a luxury necessitating some capital and a steady income in order to set up a home and maintain offspring. The nation's economic improvement undoubtedly accounts for the lower age at which British men and women marry. The average age for spinsters dropped from 25·6 in 1901 to 22·7 in 1968, with the comparable figures for bachelors 27·2 and 24·7. As notable is the large number of very young brides. The proportion of girls marrying at ages 16-18 has gone up $3\frac{1}{2}$ times during the present century.

The popularity of monogamy, established with all the public trappings of a wedding ceremony, special costume, the plaudits of relatives and friends, commemorative photographs, and the sexual rituals of the honeymoon, appears to compete successfully with the ostensibly tempting alternatives for the satisfaction of the sexual drive, and to a lesser extent, with ideas for the better organisation of the rearing and care of offspring. Human hope fortunately blinds these young modern couples to the fact that they pledge themselves to a life pattern the like of which the mass of people have never previously attempted. Mating exclusively with one person for life has, of course, been the ideal of most advanced societies in both classical and modern times. For most of the Christian era the ideal has been supported by religious and secular laws, with penalties of varying efficacy for those who broke them. Today the taboos of religion have either been relaxed or can be rejected and ignored without any risk of punishment.   *divorce cause.*

Modern newly married couples have the prospect of fifty to sixty years of life together, and are supposed to remain faithful from the wedding till death. It is a way of life which would have intimidated their ancestors. The marrying age in medieval and later centuries is often regarded as very low because of records of child betrothals of heirs to the throne and similarly socially important boys and girls. Apart from the fact that these marriages were usually formalities, remaining unconsummated till much later, they were exceptions to the wedding customs of the mass of people, particularly as regards the menfolk. Until what may be regarded as modern times even those marrying at the beginning of adult life could not expect both partners would survive for more than twenty-five years. From examination of skeletons, details on tombs and in documents, etc, it has been calculated that the average male of fifteen, safely past the killer diseases of childhood, lived to an age of thirty-one to forty years in the case of pre-historic man; to thirty-six in Athens and Rome; to about fifty in England of the fifteenth-seventeenth centuries.[4] Women, through the dangers of childbirth, did not survive so long.

It is therefore hardly surprising that, given the facilities to terminate one marriage and begin another, divorce has become a built-in escape clause in the wedding ceremony for couples who nevertheless hope they will never have to make use of it. Prior to the Reformation the civil courts of England had no power to grant a divorce. Thereafter, until 1857, a decree was possible only by a private Act of Parliament, which was a Protestant substitute for a Papal decree of dissolution. The subsequent reforms of 1923 (making the treatment of men and women similar and introducing desertion for three years as grounds for divorce), 1937 (when adultery, cruelty, and desertion became the main matrimonial offences), and 1971 (with an end to the branding of one spouse as guilty and the other as innocent and permitting divorce after five years separation even if one spouse objects to it) marked the move of the State into control of customs originally the exclusive concern of the Church. In the USA divorce laws of course vary from state to state, but significantly New York State has recently permitted divorce where husband and wife have separated, under written agreement, for a mere two years. In California, Florida, New Jersey and New Hampshire one of the partners can simply go to court and ask for a dissolution on the grounds of 'irreconcilable differences'. There is little likelihood of this trend towards regarding marriage as a secular contract between two people instead of a sacrament being reversed. A major defeat of the Catholic Church came with the 1970 legislation in Italy permitting divorce, in the face of angry and vigorous protests, both on the grounds of dogma and political agreement, by the Vatican.

On the eve of the introduction of unilateral divorce in Britain on 1 January 1971, divorce petitions in England and Wales were running at about 65,000 a year; in the United States, in 1970, at 715,000. In the span of thirty years which provide a contrast with pre-war and post-war mores, decrees made absolute in Britain increased nearly seven times: 3,668 in 1931 and 24,936 in 1961. Seven years later, in 1968, there was a further increase to 49,794.[5] Indirectly the State has been encouraging divorce. The massive increase in decrees in 1961 and afterwards was not due to a sudden collapse of moral standards but to the more generous regulations as regards legal aid, making divorce part of the State's welfare service.

The State, in its wisdom and with a commendable desire to ensure that there is equality before the law for every citizen, has almost entirely abolished obstacles imposed by religious belief, poverty, or the resistance of the 'innocent' partner. The reforms operating since the beginning of 1971 have extended the facilities for getting a divorce to virtually anyone who has been married for a sufficient number of years, irrespective of status, wealth, marital virtue or vice.

Nearly a third of modern divorces are granted to couples married between five and nine years—victims of the notorious 'seven years itch'; the next largest group, nearly a fifth of the total, have been married for twenty years and more—couples of mature years who perhaps make the break once a sense of duty towards the upbringing of their children has ended or who have at last faced the fact that whatever once made their marriage purposeful has disappeared.

The rigidity of the Churches has been steadily easing for many years. The asceticism of early Christianity had only a minor influence on European attitudes to divorce in the first centuries of the Christian era. Under the Emperor Constantine a marriage could be dissolved on the grounds of adultery or serious crime. Justinian increased the number of grounds, significantly including plotting against the Empire. The political ascendancy of the Church steadily enforced the dogma of the indissolubility of marriage throughout Europe, the only exceptions being that, as Christ taught, a man might put away his wife for fornication, and under the Pauline teaching, a Christian married to an unbeliever who deserted the marital home was no longer bound by marriage vows. In neither case, however, was re-marriage allowed.

For centuries this rigidity remained virtually inviolate—at least in theory if not always in practice. The subsequent relaxation of the Churches' attitude to divorce and re-marriage has been in direct ratio to the growth of the State's influence on the personal life of its subjects, and in the ritualistic battle of secularism versus religion, the Churches have been forced to compromise. The Church of England abandoned the traditional notion of marital sin in 1966 when its report, *Putting Asunder*, recommended that matrimonial offences should not be the grounds for a divorce, but instead it should be granted on the irretrievable breakdown of the marriage. Thus a married partner who broke the seventh commandment was no longer to be regarded as an unforgivable violator of the marriage vow. Couples who asked the State to terminate their

union were not sinners, but victims. Britain's Divorce Reform
Act which came into force in 1971 was largely the State's
agreement with this religious view. In the majority of cases of
divorce today no offence exists because an offence, as a reason
for ending a marriage, is no longer considered. Divorce has
thus become socially respectable.

The marriage laws of most western countries are not
mainly concerned with the teachings of Christ or the views
of St Paul, but are preoccupied with the rights of family
property, the welfare of the partners and their children, and
the stability of the nation's social life. The approval, or at
least the acquiescence, of the Church as regards the secular
procedure for ending marriages has made divorce feasible in
groups where once religious beliefs and social conventions
made it impossible. As a consequence, divorce—and usually
re-marriage—is no longer a hindrance to a career or social
life. Government ministers, doctors, judges, and members of
professions in which marital infringements of the marriage
code once meant ruin, are now quite unaffected. There remain the defences of the Catholic Church against the assaults
on lifelong monogamy, but even these are beginning to
crumble. The implacable dismissal of divorce as ever permissible under Vatican dogma is now subject to provisos,
exceptions, and a growing wave of criticism.

In principle the Papacy recognises civil divorce (but not re-
marriage) of Catholics only when they have been authorised
to live apart from their marital partners by the ecclesiastical
courts. For those who wish to remain in the Church and re-
marry the only procedure has been to obtain a declaration of
nullity from a Church tribunal. Until the present time this
procedure was so involved and prolonged that only the
wealthy and the extremely persistent were able to make use of
it. Signs of a compromise in the Papacy's attitudes to broken
marriage began in the summer of 1970 when, with understandably little publicity, the Vatican agreed that in the USA,
as an experiment, the lengthy ritual of the annulment hearings

B

could be simplified. One judge could hear the case instead of three, and a second trial would no longer be mandatory. This experimental change was in effect made permanent, and applied to Catholics the world over with the Pope's *motu proprio* (a personal Papal initiative) in June 1971, reducing the waiting period for an annulment hearing to a few months, with one court dealing with the evidence instead of two, as was usually the case in previous hearings.

A handful of Catholic countries permit no way of ending a marriage except through the Church's procedure of annulment. In the rest of the world civil divorce is possible, and obviously thousands of Catholics resort to the civil courts to obtain their freedom, and each thereby challenges the authority of the Church. The response has been a slight change in the attitude of some members of the Catholic hierarchy, notably in the USA. Monsignor Kelleher, a judge in the marriage court of the archdiocese of New York, stated publicly in 1968 that in some circumstances a man or woman should be given the freedom of conscience to divorce and re-marry—and still remain a communicant.

Objectively, changes in traditional family patterns due to the prevalence of divorce are of smaller impact on society than the great increase in one-parent families. Divorce usually creates a new monogamous unit of conventional type to succeed that which is destroyed. The one-parent family was previously a 'rogue' circumstance to be remedied, ostracised, or concealed. Its rarity as an enduring complement of society made it a social problem. Its present prevalence has not minimised the extent of the problem, but has resulted in the one-parent group creating its own niche in society.

One in thirteen of the babies starting life in the seventh decade of twentieth-century England and Wales was born out of wedlock. The percentage of illegitimate births was 8·4 in 1968, exactly double the figure for 1901. The rapid increase did not begin until the mid-sixties, indicating that this was a result of the so-called sexual revolution in the permissive society, and not symptomatic of insecure conditions as in the years of world wars. (It is worth noting, however, that the proportion of recorded illegitimate births most nearly approaching the present one occurred during the zenith of the Victorian puritanism, when records were first kept, in the years 1870-72.)[6]

With 65,000 to 70,000 British children born out of wedlock every year, and around 340,000 each year in the United States, the fatherless family has become a normal feature of life. Morality apart, these mother-and-baby units face basically the same practical problems as those of deserted and widowed mothers. The State therefore collates them as 'lone parent families with mother'. In 1966 they numbered more than a million and have increased since then.[7] Thus between seven and eight out of every hundred families in Britain are without male presence or supervision, though the State acts as a rather inefficient paternal substitute. Official action has, however, ensured that the unmarried mother and her offspring have the right to participate in the social services provided for all citizens—a situation indicating the growing tolerance of society to the unwed mother and her child, and a decline in emotive hostility and the temptation to pretend the problem is non-existent by ignoring it.

The more intelligent sections of society have begun to accept that the unmarried mother is not necessarily promiscuous, an irresponsible teenager, or a poverty-stricken moron. The late twentieth-century's unmarried mothers are anything from eleven to fifty years old. The peak age for unwed motherhood birth in both Britain and the United States is nineteen, and the most numerous age group is 20-24. An increasing number of unmarried mothers are in the higher social and economic groups, and nearly a third of children born out of wedlock are born to women who are in fact married but the father of the child is not the husband.

The reason that the percentage of illegitimate births is not far higher than it is must be because contraceptives are already available to the resourceful girl or considerate man, and not because the numbers indulging in extra-marital intercourse are low. To the young a meaningful relationship is a euphemism for sexual intimacy which is nevertheless an honestly held opinion of what an affectionate partnership should permit. This is not necessarily evidence of any decline in self-respect or even in personal moral values. Today's young men do not resort to prostitutes as teachers in their sexual education as their fathers and grandfathers did. A youth who is known to sleep with prostitutes is regarded with pity by his contemporaries because he is admitting his lack of success with girls in his social circle.

The girl of earlier generations repressed her own sexual desire and resisted male advances largely through fear of pregnancy, fear of being a social outcast, fear of venereal disease, and fear of hell fire. Her descendant can avoid pregnancy if she is sensible, but she knows that if she 'slips up' an unmarried mother and her baby are no longer figures of tragic horror. Although venereal diseases are rampant she knows they can be cured and that treatment under conditions of secrecy is freely available. As regards divine punishment, only a minority believe in a future hell and in any event extra-marital sex is not regarded as a sin likely to result in such a condign punishment.

Although the unmarried mother still faces appalling difficulties in creating a home, earning her living, and maintaining the traditional routines of motherhood, the position of her child and herself has slowly improved. After 1925 illegitimate children in Britain could be legitimised by the subsequent marriage of the parents, provided that they were free to marry at the time of the births; this civic status was extended to a far larger number of children in 1959, with their legitimisation on the subsequent marriage of the parents whatever their marital status at the time of the child's birth. But the stigma of being born out of wedlock—a relic of the old hatred and suspicion of the 'fruit of sexual sin'—remains while the term 'illegitimate' is unjustly and callously used for a person who has himself done nothing unlawful in being born to an unmarried woman. However, as a citizen the modern illegitimate child enjoys rights which are very nearly equal to those of everyone else, though it is doubtful whether even today he can compete on equal terms in some professions where rigorous investigation of antecedents is normal, such as in the diplomatic and the security services.

Modern society has modified its attitude to the unmarried father. The old absurdity of the child not being regarded as the offspring of his biological father, even if he co-operated with the mother at the registration of birth and had his name included on the certificate, survives. But public and personal acknowledgement of paternal rights and privileges has been possible since 1959, with the father's right to ask the State to grant him access to his child, and, if the child's interests allow, custody as well.

Complete social integration of the unmarried mother-and-child family unit is still a long way off, but it is beginning. Local authorities are—albeit grudgingly in most cases—accepting unmarried mothers on council housing lists.[8] Charitable and mutual-benefit housing trusts have come into existence to provide rented accommodation for them, unfortunately usually only for a short term. There are also scores of schemes to provide flatlets on a permanent basis. A more humane and sensible trend is to group fatherless families together so that child care can be provided on a communal basis. A social danger in this idea is the segregation from the community's life for a group which might then be regarded as suffering ostracism for its moral lapse. This danger is minimised if the group consists of fatherless families of all kinds, whether the reason is bereavement, desertion, divorce, or failure to marry. In view of the fact that there are more than a million one-parent (mother) families in Britain today, and over 5 million in the United States, this facet of the modern family pattern has to be accepted as part of the community which must affect the overall social pattern.

The birth of children to unmarried women, despite the availability of contraceptives and the possibility of abortion, is of course often due to the age-old irresponsibility and treachery of the seducing male, to ignorance, and to fecklessness. But the unmarried mother, voluntarily or through circumstance, is an exemplar of the new campaign for feminine freedom. The women's liberation campaign now flourishing in all Western countries is a curious mixture of politics, feminism and sexuality. In the USA, as among the imitators in Britain, the typical founder members are well educated, reasonably well off, married or divorced, and in the 21-30 years age-group. They are, in short, type-cast women of an affluent, democratic society. Equipped intellectually to occupy their time purposefully, married or once-married to a man of their own unrestricted choice, spared from financial worries and most of the more dreary chores of a household, they would appear to have every reason to be satisfied with a monogamous, independent family existence.

That they are not is perhaps one of the most profound pointers to the danger which today hovers over the traditional family structure, for women have the real power to make or break the spirit and meaning of marriage no matter what men may attempt to enforce by law, custom, or religion.

Politically the women's liberation movement pursues radical objectives. The feminist angle is part of the sexual revolution. Behind the call for equality of opportunity in jobs and civil life there is the suggestion, not of sex equality, but of female dominance. It is difficult to see how rejection of a society based on male-female units in a separate sub-culture for each sex, with temporary alliances carrying no responsibilities on either side, can result in anything but social anarchy, and this human beings, eager for security, never pursue for very long. The more extreme ideas of women's liberation, implying isolation of the sexes except for biological needs, is so great a divergence from human behaviour patterns that it must remain a minority movement, probably fading away once the more reasonable objectives of equality in work and law have been reached.

Far more significant as regards the relationship between men and women is the blurring of sex differences and roles. Modern civilisation favours the unisex citizen. Machines continue to minimise the need for masculine strength in work, and the same machines are increasing the opportunities for women eager to prove they can do a man's job. Equal pay and equal opportunity in employment, already the aim of women and the promise of men, are close to becoming realities among the Western industrial nations, while the so-called emergent nations have already turned their women into soldiers and are giving them opportunities in government. A teenage generation which adopted inter-sex clothing—jeans, sweaters, T-shirts, hippy costume—are unlikely ever to revert to dress which is completely exclusive to one sex. Deodorants, shampoos, and some cosmetics are unisex, and recreation and sport are becoming more mixed.

The mingling of activities previously restricted to one sex has encouraged an easy-going companionship for men and women. The result has been to de-glamorise sexual relationships and, indeed, to push them into the background. The jealousy and intense passions hitherto regarded as proofs of love are largely absent. This rather emotionless way of life makes it possible for comparatively large groups of both sexes to live in close intimacy without hostility. Challenged to name the type of family existence which could replace the present private two-persons foundation, young adults will usually suggest the commune. This is an important revolutionary development of today's family life, having regard to its widespread adoption and the serious determination of its members to make it work. Criticism of the practice is invariably motivated by emotional prejudice and a misconception of the objectives of the more responsible communes. The groups of young drop-outs from society who combine for self-protection and for sexual promiscuity, squatting in 'derries' (derelict buildings), or adopting a nomadic existence, are by their nature ephemeral and of no more significance than any other haphazard grouping based mainly on sexual interest.

The communes of young people who have deliberately opted out, as distinct from dropping out, from a social structure they regard as bad have a far stronger basis. The sexual impetus is subsidiary to the social aim. Intentionally permanent pairings of the members are respected. Rules as regards co-operative effort are usually enforced by the threat of expulsion from the group for their infringement. The only valid criticism (which, of course, the members would reject) is that the commune's mores do not demand legalisation of a pairing, and the occasional sexual adventure cannot therefore be adultery, and is tolerated. This degree of sexual freedom is balanced against the restrictions imposed by group living.

In this form, especially when the sexual relationship of one male and one female member is more or less permanent, the idea of the commune is not particularly new. Apart from experiments by Victorian romantics and practitioners of an idealised form of Socialism, communal family life offered a practical solution of the housing problem immediately after the end of the second world war. Young married couples, accustomed to living in a minimum of privacy while in the services, amalgamated with their contemporaries and were able to purchase a large house more easily than a small one. Most of these communes broke up as soon as conventional accommodation became easier to obtain, and the increased wealth of the members enabled them to move out.

The more modern communes of young people are usually founded through a wish to escape from the conventional family structure and all the social conditions which stem from it. The young men and women in them are invariably refugees from homes they disliked and the members have to some degree severed connection with their parents. Communes which are managing to survive do so because the wishes of the individual are subject to the approval or disapproval of the group—usually to a far greater extent than is the practice in the conventional family structure. The discipline is accepted because of the common ambition of all its members to further some interest, be it a religious cult, abolition of capitalist practices, or observance of dietary rules. As a result the successful communes are developing on lines which were familiar in the original and stable families and clans of primitive societies. They prefer isolation from allegedly hostile groups around them, either by establishing their dwelling places in remote rural areas, as is possible in the USA, or in districts of towns and cities due for demolition, and deserted by conventional society, as in Britain.

Their defect as compared with primitive communal groups is that the members are too alike. Interests are almost identical, there is only one age group, and the group is classless. The revolt against the society which the commune members have left creates a new and invariably quite as strict an array of conventions and taboos.

At the same time the modern commune is unconsciously reviving many of the best features of primitive family life. Those which have been established in rural areas and are endeavouring to become self-sufficient have a commendable regard for the benefits of honest toil, believe in mutual assistance in times of sickness and other personal crises, and try to put the welfare of the group before personal aggrandisement. It has been grudgingly conceded by social workers that the children in the communes are well adjusted and happy, thanks to the freedom from the repressions of a class-conscious acquisitive society, and particularly because many adults are always present and all take on the role of parents in so far as communication, play, and constant care are concerned.

In the West it is the nature of communes to be politically opposed to the economy and society in which they are struggling to exist. As such they are bound to arouse some suspicion and hostility among the majority of the population. Whether they develop so as to become an accepted way of life will depend on the tenacity of the present commune members to hold on, or, as they would hope, that their qualities set such an example that they will trigger off a social revolution and eventually become a widely adopted and almost conventional form of family existence.

When such communes emerge as a State-approved social experiment their potentialities for progress and development are impressive, as exemplified in the kibbutzim of Israel. The first kibbutz was founded as long ago as 1910 at Degania on land at the southern end of Lake Tiberias (Sea of Galilee) in the Jordan valley by ten young men and two women. By the 1970s there were 235 kibbutzim, with members ranging from fifty to more than a thousand, and making a total of 85,000, about 3.5 per cent of the Israeli population.[9] Based originally on theories brought by Jewish refugees from Russia from the teachings of Tolstoy on mutual labour and the sharing of possessions, the basic precepts are that there shall be no preferential treatment for the individual and complete equality of duty and privilege. A new member is accepted after a year on probation. There is no private property apart from a few personal possessions. A committee assigns work and ensures that everyone's needs are fairly met from the available resources. Women enjoy equal rights, and while their children are housed in quarters specially designed for them, they are not really separated from their parents, and the warmth and affection of the Jewish family remain untouched.

The immigrants who poured in after 1948, many no longer young, found the pattern of family life in the kibbutzim incomprehensible rather than odious. These new Israelis adapted the kibbutz to the moshav, in which a member lives in a house of his own and farms for himself on a holding which is the same size as the other members of the commune. A council and various specialised committees organise all facets of life in the moshav so far as general policy is concerned. This modification of the kibbutz idea permits some retention of the traditional Jewish custom of patriarchy in family life, though it should be stressed that Israel practises sex equality, both within and outside the kibbutzim, on a scale rarely found in any other State.

The Israeli commune has been moulded by considerations of patriotism and political theory. Its objectives have been in tune with the State and not against its interests. The strictly monogamous pattern of mating has been maintained, thanks to the vigour of religious beliefs and the precise teachings which the Jewish religion provides. Sexual mores remain the same as in any other Jewish community, though the patriarchal force is weaker. The major family contrast is the communal care of children, with parental influence thereby weakened. Time has proved that this is no bad thing.

It would be risky to forecast that the communal family idea will develop as a viable solution of the problem of retaining some kind of personal affinity in societies consisting of millions of people, politically and ideologically allied to more millions. But of all the possible successors to the patterns of family life which are now apparently in process of decline, or at least change, the commune can be supported on every responsible plane—morally, socially, and economically. What is certain is that it is not a revolutionary and entirely novel concept of a pattern of living. No matter what idea for human partnership is conceived one may be assured of discovering that it has been tried before. None of them has been an unqualified success, and none a complete failure.

Edmund Burke said that society was a partnership between those who were living, those who were dead, and those yet to be born. The interests of each generation cannot unexceptionally coincide, so that the adopted pattern must always be a compromise of self-interest, duty, instinctive desire, and the taboos and conventions of civilisation. Basically the challenge facing twentieth century men and women is little different from that which the first-born of mankind met and overcame in the early hesitant steps towards a social existence.

Notes and Bibliography for this chapter are on pp169-70.

2 *Birth of the Human Family*

Arguments in support of a particular type of family structure usually include a claim that it is natural, the product of human instinct, ignoring the biological view that the higher the intelligence of an animal the less it depends on instinct for self-preservation. In fact virtually all human activities, however natural and automatic they may seem to be, are the result of learning, with the exceptions of the sucking instinct and the fear of falling.

Behaviour patterns are part of evolution. In time some of them became fixed throughout a species. But many kinds of behaviour are the result of adapting to the conditions of environment, climate and so on. These, when proved of value by the fact that the animals adopting them survive and multiply, are repeatedly adopted by each generation, largely by imitation of parents and other members of the species. The nervous system of human beings is so complex, so much the product of aeons of time after communication from one generation to the next had become highly efficient, that identification of the type of behaviour pattern is difficult and debatable. But there can be no denial that the human capacity for learning is as uniquely developed as his inborn behaviour patterns are few. As a result his way of doing things can be flexible, while the lower animals, however elaborate their nest or lair building, courtship, care of offspring, and so on may be, are dependent on inborn rules which they cannot ignore and which survive unaltered in a particular species.

It must be difficult to claim that any type of human family structure is based on natural laws which man will infringe at his peril. It is quite impossible to obtain evidence on what type of family first proved successful among humanity's ancestors, or the degree to which the first hominids were subject to natural laws implanted as instincts because their intelligence was insufficiently developed.

In the hostile world in which the hominid emerged one presumes that he experienced the two emotions common to all wild animals: sex hunger and fear. The former created the pugnacity of the male, the acquiescence of the female, and the mating of both. The latter drove both sexes to experiments on the best way to survive. Evolution demanded that man, like all creatures, experimented. Failure meant extinction; success, survival with offspring to imitate parental behaviour.

As the creature which was to become man began to develop about two million years ago, even the physiological data about this early anthropoid must be theoretical. Sexual interest may have occurred only seasonally, maturation occupying fewer years, the life span much briefer than in contemporary man. But the changes in a creature of roughly human stature and weight, and normally producing only one offspring at a birth, when compared with the biology of modern man, must be comparatively slight and of no significance in a study of family development.

One may safely assume, therefore, that these remote near-ancestors experienced roughly the same problems in maintaining the species as ourselves: a long period of gestation, offspring completely helpless for up to a year, incapable of effective agility for eighteen months to two years, and not adult for at least a dozen years after that.

The obstacles in rearing this fragile form of life were too formidable for an indeterminate number of these evolutionary try-outs towards a uniquely intelligent mammal, and they died out. The victors were those who maintained some kind of long-term cohesion between food-getting male, breeding female, and developing young, or just possibly there were females of remarkable resourcefulness who, against all the odds, somehow independently fed themselves and cared for their young long past the three or four years of lactation.

It is an interesting though easily misleading study to look at the behaviour of existing animals which may be regarded as the descendants of the early travellers on much the same route as man. This infers a static situation over hundreds of thousands of generations, irrespective of climate, evolution and adaptability—clearly a source of erroneous conclusions. In any event the habits and customs of the primates are so varied that virtually any desired theory about early anthropoid behaviour can be happily adopted if the contradictory evidence ascertainable from other species is ignored.

The gibbon, sexually and anatomically fairly similar to modern man, is mostly monogamous, mainly because the female gibbon is, like the human female, always ready to be sexually co-operative. The male gibbon can therefore regularly assuage his sexual hunger with one mate and has little need to seek out another, while the female always has a motive to drive off other females. But the gibbon is a gregarious animal and mating fidelity can be strained beyond breaking point if conditions create too much congestion and a food shortage.

In other primate groups the nuclear family pattern is constantly broken. Baboons live in clans of twenty or more. A handful of adult males each has three or four wives who are guarded from any sexual approach by any male not in the

'club'. Young males are ignored until they start to approach
the married females, when they are driven off. They lurk in
the vicinity of the adults and may become homosexual until
they can pair with young females who in their turn are
driven out by the adult females because of the approach of
the adult males to the newly sexually attractive baboons. The
howler monkeys of South America present a rough replica of
a modern human community living in close proximity in a
hamlet or, perhaps, a block of flats. Groups may total a hundred and more, with the sexes only by accident roughly
equally divided. The female howlers are fertile for two or
three days in every twenty-eight. Only at that period are they
sexually attractive and permit coitus. Observations show
that the fertile period is different for each female so that in
a group of forty or so females there is never a time when
four or five are not sexually receptive. At this time these
females will copulate with every male in the group. There is
a degree of mild rivalry among the males but no definite
attack once a female has begun to submit. Gorillas and chimpanzees have a social system where masculinity and age
confer the usual benefits of leadership, and it is noteworthy
that the gorilla leaders exert authority which is benign. They
rarely resort to physical violence to maintain order. Females
who are not sexually active and the young play around them
and approach for security and comforting. Both gorillas and
chimpanzees copulate apparently indiscriminately, and permanent pairings do not seem to exist.

The variety of sexual and social behaviour of all these
species is so great that it is clearly the result of aeons of
making the best of a given situation. Climate, terrain, food
supplies, dangers from other animals—all help to decide the
size of the group and its social order. Nor is there much
validity in imagining that the origins of human marriage and
family customs can be ascertained by quoting those much
investigated survivors of primitive life in the mountains of
New Guinea, the remoter areas of South America, and the

Australian bush. However 'backward' these people may have been until the last century or so, they are the products of successful experiment and change bringing some sort of progress, or they would have been wiped out in the early dawn of history. Evolution may occur at different speeds; it cannot come completely to a stop.

That some early anthropoids devised some sort of plan for mating and rearing children, by deliberate action rather than natural compulsion, must have been forced on them by exterior influences. Climate must have been one of the most important, for in the two million years since near-man emerged, and the hundred thousand years which have passed since *homo sapiens* developed, there have been climatic changes which represented an ultimatum to him: adapt or die. So far as the northern hemisphere is concerned four great glacial ages, separated by interglacial periods, caused the movement of plants and animals as hapless puppets of the climate. In Europe the ice age starting about 600,000 years ago, probably saw the creatures which were to develop into humans fleeing southwards to more temperate zones. Both man-like creatures and lesser animals which lacked either the intelligence or the physical ability to migrate succumbed.[1]

But some hominids had by then developed both intelligence and mobility. As forest and jungle gave way to treeless plains what was probably a tree-haunting animal, existing almost entirely above ground level, using all four limbs for fast, safe movement, descended and became a ground animal, walking almost erect and rarely relying on the forelimbs for movement. His eyes were already placed in the front of the skull, giving him bi-focal vision, valuable for gauging distance and size, but a defect as regards registering the presence of enemies to the side; so the head had to be kept truly erect and capable of quick movement from side to side.

An erect posture left the forelimbs free to handle missiles,

C

tools and weapons. By using stones and pieces of wood or bone the hominids equipped themselves with an extension of the limb and an additional protection. This intelligent use of artificial additions to his body was essential because the hominid had become extremely vulnerable. His ground existence was much more dangerous than in his tree habitat. His body had little protective covering; his movement was slower than predators and quarries of much the same size as himself; his strength was poor compared with the large, slow moving animals which both menaced him and were a valuable source of food.

Survival without some kind of co-operative effort among hominids would appear unlikely. A developing brain and the constant proximity of his fellows encouraged ingenuity. The making of tools—a tremendous advance on merely using them—suggests that intelligible speech was emerging: the hominids needed to name objects and later to describe them so as to convey information from one member of the group to another, and to instruct the young. Tool making also indicates an awareness of future needs. It is one thing to pick up a handy stone or stick when confronting an animal; quite another to equip oneself for an attack planned for the following day.

Slender evidence of the way of life of hominids in the latter phases of the Pleistocene period, some 400,000 years ago, comes from the remains found at Chou K'ou Tien, the site where Peking man, *Sinanthropus*, lived.[2] He was a hunter, eating large quantities of meat whatever other forms of food he used to supplement the diet. This valuable form of protein, nourishing him adequately in widely spaced meals instead of his having interminably to eat every waking hour, as is necessary for vegetarian animals, left him time to develop his tool-making skills and, maybe, deliberately to organise some sort of social grouping.

Peking man was a very skilful hunter. The bones on the site included those of wild pig, wild horse, deer, antelope, buffalo, elephant, rhinoceros, and predatory carnivorae. He managed to kill and butcher these animals after dragging the carcases to his settlement, by using crude tools, such as stones broken by crushing to produce shards with sharp edges, and bones deliberately broken to create a sharp end at the fracture. All these ingenious accessories for survival pale into insignificance compared with his creation and use of fire, which in that area is all the more remarkable because spark-producing stones are not easily found. It therefore seems more likely that Peking man had discovered how friction between two slivers of wood created fire—a patient, single-minded activity denoting the ability to discipline the brain to achieve an end not evident without experience or information. Fire was difficult to create and had to be carefully nurtured, which for creatures engaged in long hunting forays this infers the static occupation of some members of the group as fire tenders. The female was perhaps getting her first role as a contributing member of the group.

The Peking dig yielded remains of forty-five hominids. How many were numbered in the group at any one time or how many generations are represented by these remains cannot be estimated. The human bones were just part of the general food debris. The larger bones had been deliberately broken, not to make tools, but to extract the marrow and, in the case of the skull the brains. Peking man was a cannibal. None of the bones gave any hint of another type of near-human, so this was not the site of a superior species catching and eating an inferior one. The members of the species ate each other, either because they were strangers caught and killed somewhere in the hunting area or—and these creatures were probably carrion eaters when they fortuitously came across a large dead animal— simply because they had a corpse of one of the group to augment the day's food foray. In such a ruthless social grouping offspring would have needed fierce protection, and a female some kind of defence if her mate was to have her exclusively for himself. The group's survival in hunting could hardly have been achieved without co-operative effort by several males excavating pits as traps, flushing out game and driving it towards weapon-carrying comrades, organising concerted attacks on the larger and more dangerous animals, and carrying the heavy carcases back to the settlement. This co-operation surely extended to mutual respect as regards the mated females.

Sinanthropus had marched a long way on the evolutionary road compared with his ancestor who came down from the trees. His brain was nearly twice as large as that of *Australopithecus*, traces of whom have been found in East Africa. Relics of about a hundred of these near-men have been discovered—relics of a creature intelligent enough to use the cunning of his brain to compensate for his physical defects in the harsh world he inhabited. But he seems to have been a loner, wandering, perhaps occasionally with a mate, in the interminable search for food, knowing little if anything of the safety of organised grouping, and being killed or creeping away to die, unmourned and unknown. His concept of family —or lack of it—spelt his doom.

Mastery over circumstance and environment improved when creatures like Peking man recognised that there had to be some stability in life. Probably neither the male nor the female hominid was consciously aware that the act of copulation would result in the birth of a baby nine months later, so it is unlikely that the adult male would have had any compulsion to form a pair-bond. On the contrary, his almost insatiable sex hunger and desire for sexual conquest would have urged him to seek a new mate. Only when advancing pregnancy restricted a female's ability to seek her own food and search for grubs and berries would she have had a motive for persuading a male to look after her. This dependence obviously became essential for several days after the birth of her baby, and to a lesser extent for up to two years while the peculiarly helpless kind of offspring she had borne restricted her own hunting and foraging activities.

A degree of permanence thus entered into the behaviour pattern. There was probably a monogamous relationship, at least for a few months, for even if the evidence of lifelong monogamy among some animals and birds is outweighed by innumerable examples of separation and change in partner-ships there is an almost universal protective pattern which transcends the basic sexual attraction. Lions remain in the pride after the cubs are born and for long periods make no sexual approach to the lioness; male birds help to re-build nests and hatch and feed the young after the mating period is over. The 'instinct' for the survival of the species has appar-ently inculcated the necessity for this sort of co-operative duty by the male and female parents. The hominid, with his superior intelligence, could work out why it was advantageous.

Early man was becoming conscious of the passage of time, not merely as a change in the seasons triggering off animal activities such as food storage, change in coat or plumage, migration, hibernation and so on, but with an assessment of the future and a memory which heeded the lessons of the past. The female knew from experience and communication with other females that the cessation of menstruation and the swell-ing of her breasts and belly were indications that she would give birth to a baby by the time the current season, the sub-sequent one, and a third was at its full. Communication en-abled her to tell her mate of the coming child. Preparation for the birth was no longer that of an animal creeping away into a quiet lair but an intelligent forecast of the future.

In the battle to exist the female and her young were an additional burden for the hunting male. His intelligent, self-interested wish must have been to leave them, and doubtless he often did, with death through starvation or animal attack for the fairly helpless woman and child he left to their own devices or the half-hearted aid of other females. But more often, fortunately for the future *homo sapiens*, some impulse, perhaps with a tinge of nobility in it, kept him by his mate's side.

One may be sure that the innate ingenuity and resourcefulness of the female helped to retain his fidelity. Apart from her
sexual attraction, she made practical contributions to his well-
being. She had the time and patience to skin animals, to
fashion coverings from the skins as protection against the cold,
to learn by trial and error how to scrape away all the flesh so
that the skins did not rot too quickly, and from this experience
how to preserve meat for a few days when a big animal was
killed. She could serve her mate by guarding the lair and its
surplus food from marauders. She could keep the fire alive,
and on it she learned how to cook the meat, thus breaking
down its fibres and increasing the nutritive value of the food
and the ease with which it could be digested. The burden of
a female was at last proving to be an asset to the hunting male.

Perhaps the earliest hunting hominids lived as nomadic
solitaries, a male with one or two females and their young,
with food fairly easy to obtain from the swampy ground teem-
ing with animal and insect life. But with the gradual increase
of cold and the decline of the forests the terrain became
harsher. The animals which adapted to the change were more
fleet of foot and timorous. Co-operation by several males on
hunting forays yielded more meat, sometimes with a surplus
for later use. Thus the hunting base became the home of
several males and their mates, and wandering was restricted.

Apparently there has always been a rough equality as to the
number of male and female human offspring, with a slight increase in the number of females surviving to maturity.[3] In
these conditions a monogamous union was the most practical
one, the fertile young adults pairing off amicably. But this
ideal could be constantly spoiled. The male, as the hunter and
fighter, incurred more risks than the female. Even slight in-
juries could be fatal. Widows must have been a problem
eroding the social structure of Pleistocene men, the solution
being polygamy by the most pugnacious male in the group.

That a degree of stability in sexual relationships emerged
despite all the difficulties was a momentous step forward, not

only ensuring the numerical growth of the species but stimulating mental activity. The male began to curb his instinct to copulate with any and every female he came across, and the female, with responses easily aroused by a male, started to show some discrimination. Perhaps originally a handful of males and females copulated indiscriminately with no question of jealousy or hostility among those of the same sex. Pairing off for a considerable period, as short as that involved in finishing off a large animal or as long as the final weeks of a female's pregnancy and the first few months of her lactation, when her sexual desires were quiescent, gave a selective union a place in the order of human life. This stability of partnership minimised most of the problems of the female in protecting herself and her baby, while the male for the first time had a sense of owning, not only the female, but her baby. He was experiencing the first glimmer of what procreation and fatherhood meant.

These near-humans, Lower Paleolithic men, apparently spread over most of the old world. After at least 350,000 years —a million generations and probably many more—*homo sapiens* appeared as their evolutionary product. He was a specialised hunter, equipped with a variety of shaped missiles, an array of tools, a liking for personal ornaments, the skills to produce graphic art, and a veneration for life exemplified by his care for his dead. His mate has established herself, not merely as a helpmate, but as a figure of veneration. Some 25,000 years ago men were carving figurines of women in settlements stretching from the Caucasus to France. Breasts full of milk and abdomens swollen in pregnancy are the depicted features, and often only the lower part of the torso was portrayed.[4] Man was pondering on his life and the lives of those who would follow him. Perhaps he was still dubious about the connection between copulation and birth, for few phallic symbols have been found for this period.

The female was therefore regarded as having a near-monopoly of magical powers to produce young and to feed them from within her body; the indications of her ability to bear children and nourish them were as important as her sexual attractions. The outlines of the genitalia in these prehistoric 'Venus' figures are either omitted or vague. In fashioning symbols of female fertility man was discovering lofty ideas. Woman was a sexual companion and a workmate—an ordinary, useful creature. She was also, by masculine standards, superhuman. Adoration of the female and her inexplicable powers was akin to a religion, possibly the first and only truly world-wide religion there has ever been.

Climatic changes, so slow that none could have been noticeable in the lifetime of Upper Paleolithic man and his Mesolithic successor, were of profound influence on their existence. Cold increased steadily until about 15,000 BC. Milder conditions followed until once more cold prevailed at about 8000 BC. There followed aeons of a cool, wet climate till 5000 BC; thereafter warmth increased to 2000 BC. So far as the discovered traces of human existence show, the climatic changes occurring after 10,000 BC had the most effect on behaviour patterns. Human beings by then were numerous and ingenious enough to adapt to the changed conditions without suffering the decimation which must have occurred in previous ice ages and the intervening warm periods. In Northern and Central Europe, as the glaciers retreated and huge rivers appeared, food of animal origin was easily garnered as fish from the water or caught without much difficulty as small creatures, though cunning and agile, swarmed over the treeless land. But of even greater value as a source of food was the development of agriculture and stock-keeping.

These two skilled crafts had a profound influence on the development of family life, with the female again strengthening her position in the group. A theory beloved of feminists is that the female discovered the method of sowing seed and ultimately harvesting the crops which grew from them because, with her characteristic fidelity, she mourned for a dead mate. Thanks to her devotion a corpse was no longer so much carrion to be disposed of by leaving it where it fell or pushing it aside along with food debris, but was buried with care and respect (often beneath the surface of the dwelling so that the body remained a member of the family). The woman's belief or hope that death was not a finality meant that the corpse needed food. Fruits, nuts and berries placed on the grave eventually sprouted—to the thoughtful wonder of the mourning female. Her knowledge of the way to grow food was yet further evidence of her magical powers to create life.

A partial dependence on agriculture had further effects on stabilising the family. It selected a permanent shelter in which to live. The hunting method of livelihood had worked best with a limited number of males ranging over a wide area. Periodically the group had had to move to a new region where animals were still plentiful and not so wary. Crop growing of the most rudimentary type now necessitated a fixed habitation for the better part of a year; as many years as the land would stand before becoming exhausted. In this agricultural economy the female was promoted from her early role as a gatherer of wild food as a supplement to the meat diet to an equal partner. The actual work of sowing, tending and harvesting the crops was mainly her duty.

Dexterity, patience, ingenuity, and knowledge became as important as brute strength and fleetness of foot had been the vital qualities of the hunter. Moreover, within limits, the more persons there were working in agriculture the better, in contrast to the hunting group where eventual scarcity of game soon created difficulties if family groups became too large and numerous. The more people to work on the crops (and even tiny children could contribute) the more land could be cleared, tilled and tended, and the more food produced. Progress was potentially illimitable.

The sense of time became more important. Agriculture necessitated looking to the future—the food and seed for next season, next year, a whole lifetime ahead. Once again the female was the inspiration. For her the future had long been supremely important. She thought about it as the child grew in her womb, about the years which had to pass before the offspring could live independently, about her own welfare as she saw young and attractive females growing up around her. Agriculture gave her the chance to encourage her man to plan for the future and to work tenaciously to ensure the plans were achieved.

The pioneer farmers apparently originated in the Near East. Wild wheat and barley grew there. These people also developed stock keeping and breeding, encouraged by the presence of wild animals suitable for domestication. The mixed economy of cereal and meat production was a certain winner. Food supplies were now more evenly spread over the year; there were dried cereals which could be stored, and there were foods which provided a variety of nutritive substances never before eaten except by accident or good fortune. Despite a high concentration of human beings, all devoted to the ceaseless activity of mixed farming, these early communities do not appear to have adopted the communal type of household and marriage prevalent in later periods. The nuclear family of parents and children kept its identity by enjoying a degree of privacy, as had been the case among their ancestors.

The people of the Gravettian culture,[5] for example, who settled beside the large rivers of Southern Russia and on the plains of central Europe after the ice receded, enjoyed a lavish source of food by hunting the almost helpless mammoth and gathering the inexhaustible supplies of food in the water shallows, but as there were no caves in which to dwell they had to construct their own homes. Traces are naturally slight, but the marks of holes which held wooden posts and the debris of fires indicate that these people constructed their huts in rows or groups for defence and mutual contact, each hut of a size indicating that it provided shelter for a man, his woman, and their children.

Even the passage of time and a great increase in food

supply, with sufficient to support many hundreds, did not destroy this desire to maintain the identity of the nuclear family. At Khirokta in Cyprus there are traces of a community which existed about 5500 BC. The forty-eight huts, made from mud bricks, which have been discovered are the survivors of what may have been a village of several hundred such huts, the homes of a population of more than a thousand.

The custom of identifying the family unit by maintaining privacy for its members is vividly shown at Skara Brae in the Orkney islands, where the use of stone for the buildings and the subsequent shifting of sand to preserve the site have left ample evidence of how the occupants lived.[6] Although this Stone age village was built and inhabited by people at a much later date than that of the Neolithic development of agriculture, the people who lived at Skara Brae were so far from the mainstream of human progress that their way of life was many centuries behind that of those living in more fertile areas. The community appears to have consisted of about half a dozen families totalling thirty or forty people. Each house had one large room measuring about 18 x 20ft, with a fire in the centre and niches in the walls for the storage of food, bedding, and tools, and possibly to serve as cots for children. The houses are basically identical in size, indicating that irrespective of the number of children or the status of the adult male, dwelling privileges were the same for all.

In favourable areas, with little or no competition for land and hunting territory from other groups of men the early custom of the lone hunter, with his mate and young, could linger on. Some finds have been made of isolated dwellings with absolutely no trace of any dwelling in the vicinity. As late as the Early Iron Age single family dwellings are found in widely scattered areas in Europe. The traces of a conical hut protected by a roughly circular fence at Little Woodbury, Wiltshire, are typical.

This isolation was neither productive of lavish food supplies nor of stimulation for better ideas. Those were the assets of people living in unusually fertile areas which attracted settlers. By 4000 BC progress along the fertile banks of the Tigris and Euphrates was so great that civilisation had begun. The soil was so fertile that there was no need to move every year from exhausted land and the farming families remained static for generations.

More food meant more children. More children meant more hands to cultivate more land. Children, and the female who produced them, were priceless assets. Marriage was no longer motivated solely by sexual desire, but adopted as part of a plan to achieve prosperity both for the individual and the group. The arranged union, with little or no consideration for the feelings of the couple involved, was emerging as a corner stone of the family structure. A virgin was a valuable asset to her father and indirectly to the clan of which he was a member. If a man from a neighbouring group wanted a mate and could approach the girl's community in peace he had to compensate her family if they were to lose her. Only after generations of civilisation had produced inheritable wealth could young men possibly hand over anything valuable enough to compensate for the potential work of the girl and the value of the children she would bear. A male stranger's best chance of obtaining a mate was to join the girl's clan and work on its behalf.

Purchase of a wife by service to her family meant that, usually for his entire life, the incoming male remained a second-grade member of the clan. His presence was tolerated because he was paying for clan membership with work and by fathering children, who would be members of his wife's clan, not of his, which he had abandoned on marriage. Within the marital home he may well have enjoyed the traditional role of being the dominant partner, his wife obeying him as regards the work she did, but so far as the wife's relatives and her clan were concerned he was a subservient worker and the inferior of his wife.

This contempt for the strange male, paralleled by the

veneration of the female he married, evidently became extreme in groups where the clannishness was very strong. The Iroquois Indians of North America, subjected to careful study before the decline of the six tribes which comprised the confederation, are regarded as having the highest form of government and social order of any of the indigenous people of the New World north of Mexico. Prior to the influence of missionaries and the effects of wars between the tribes and with the white invaders, the Iroquois male who came from another clan in search of a wife was tolerated only for his breeding capabilities. He was not allowed to live in the territory of his wife's clan but remained in his mother's (not his father's) lodge, obtaining permission to visit his wife on occasions which the older women considered favourable for conception. Apart from these visits for supervised sexual intercourse he was expected to make brief but regular calls at his wife's lodge to present her family with gifts of food. Failure to keep up the food supply or to father a child could result in divorce. The husband had no rights over his children and indeed was rarely permitted to see them.

Denigration of the status of the 'foreign' male on this scale could occur only when the wife's clan was extremely prosperous and strong, and the clan of the husband correspondingly weak. The imbalance could only be temporary. The natural increase in population stimulated rivalry. The existence of a clan enjoying life in a fertile, well farmed area, obviously prospering and growing in size, was noted and envied by less fortunate groups, and defensive operations therefore became essential. Fighting had to be developed as a skill instead of the haphazard activity of the dim past.

With man permanently settled in the midst of his crops and domesticated animals, flight was no longer a feasible way of admitting defeat. Defensive war had to be fought. Adequate defences were beyond the capabilities of any diehard farmer clinging to the old system of solitary existence of a nuclear family. A clan which was rich in breeding women and children, but poor in manpower, was not of much use as a defensive unit.

Thus the growing complexity and prosperity of the farming and herding people encouraged a closer affinity among the males as the defenders of communal property. Masculine comradeship could be as strong a factor binding a group together as the ties of family relationships through ancestry. The social structure of these defended communities was therefore still based on family, but the group itself was becoming more important than the families of which it was composed.

Once the community's welfare became of paramount importance, and the breeding of children part of the community's concern in order to increase its power and wealth, the exclusiveness of marriage with sexual activities confined to one man and one wife was in jeopardy. A virile, and therefore valuable, male might be permitted or even encouraged to father children by women whose husbands were weak, injured, or for some reason poor assets. A wife who had proved her fecundity and her ability to bear healthy babies might have to submit to mating with numerous males in order to ensure conception as frequently as possible. This was not a form of promiscuity, but a deliberate attempt to enhance the quality and quantity of offspring. Man-woman relationships were, of course, beneficial as regards food preparation, home building, and child care, but the basic approval of a union was for the purpose of breeding for the benefit of the clan.

Care of domesticated animals created knowledge of the techniques of breeding. Natural selection could be assisted by culling inferior male animals and taking special care of females which produced high quality offspring, and several generations of these selected animals provided lessons in both the benefits and dangers of in-breeding. Genetic defects may take longer to appear than the qualities. It can therefore be assumed that the procedure which at first seemed so successful in breeding animals was adopted in human relationships in order to improve some such quality as strength, stature or beauty—and, of course, to confine the benefits to an identifiable family grouping. Parent-offspring and brother-sister matings were the obvious ways of producing these desirable offspring.

In a sequence of such matings recessive genes will in time show themselves. Inbreeding over several generations produces offspring of less vigour and smaller size; they are prone to die young and fertility decreases, but such deterioration is gradual, and man probably became aware of the dangers of inbreeding from more dramatic evidence, such as albinism, which to a primitive community must have been a frightening condition. Much more repellent are two abnormalities originating from recessive genes: deaf-mutism and the existence of additional or embryonic fingers (polydactyly).

Incest taboos were thus devised for practical reasons, and notions of instinctive repulsion about sexual union between members of a nuclear family cannot be supported. In a primitive community marriages which would today be regarded as incestuous must have been tolerated until taboos were devised in order to improve physique and intelligence by out-breeding and to increase the community's wealth and power by absorbing both male and female mates from neighbouring clans.

The rules about marriage—which could be very different from those designed to prohibit infringement of property rights by punishing extra-marital intercourse—were designed to ensure harmony within the group and to enhance its well-being. The conventions and taboos were therefore varied. A marriage which was forbidden in one clan might be lauded or actually enforced in another. Thus a man might be compelled to take as an additional wife the widow of his brother. In contrast incest taboos might be so complicated that marriage between members of a clan was virtually prohibited.

People who develop a close-knit community, living in the same place for generation after generation, have rarely been able to sustain a rigid practice of life-long and exclusive monogamy. One reason why this type of permanent family structure was liable to crumble was the new practice of living in a communal dwelling. It was obviously cheaper and more convenient to construct one large hut instead of a number of small ones, and the adoption of this idea was widespread and marks a notable stage in the progress of a community's social life. In such an environment sharing of sexual partners became normal. There had either to be general tolerance about it or stringent punishments with the accompanying dangers of creating dissensions and eventually breakaway groups.

Until religious laws and secular power grew sufficiently to impose laws about sexual behaviour, it was inevitable that a clan living under one roof became one large family, with the identity of sexual partners of little importance. With the maternal parent the only one who was readily identifiable, relationships among the two generations of parents and offspring became enormously complicated. Engels describes the relationships of Iroquois Indians who lived in the area of the present New York State. The adult male regarded not only the offspring of his own wife as his sons and daughters, but also those of his brothers and their wives. All these children addressed him as father. But the children of the man's sisters were regarded as nephews and nieces. An Iroquois married woman regarded both her own children and those of her sisters as her children, and they called her mother. But her brothers' children were her nephews and nieces. The children of brothers called one another brother or sister, as did those who were the children of sisters. The children born to one woman regarded the sons and daughters of their mother's brother as cousins. This elaborate system of family relationships clearly involved many absurdities, particularly as it depended on the identification of paternity with the official husband, whereas in fact the real father might have been another man in the group.

The development of trade and its accompanying wars of conquest and acquisition spelt the eventual doom of the self-contained group with membership based on closely related families. Slaves and booty were yielded from territory beyond the clan's area occupied for farming, and the trader warriors regarded their slaves and stolen goods as their personal property, or at best that of their leader. Women were again becoming second-rate members of the clan. They were the stay-at-homes who carried on the unspectacular tasks in the complex farmer-trader-warrior society. But loss of status in the general community was compensated by some gains in personal security as wife and mother. The possessive desires of the male, encouraged by the spoils of warfare and trading, were extended to his principal wife and her children. They were just items among his goods and chattels, with few personal rights, but at least could expect to be guarded as jealously as the personal slaves, the weapons, and tools as symbols of masculine prestige.

Marriage customs began to be modified to meet the new situation. The young unmarried warrior was expected to go out and capture or buy a bride, and the mere fact that he brought her back to his clan implied that his marriage was his personal affair and in any event an already established situation. The married man could gain prestige by returning with a captured girl, and the greater number of wives he could find abroad and put to work to enhance his wealth the greater his reputation in his community. As wives were no longer just sexual companions and breeders but symbols of power and wealth, to be guarded and restricted, a separate dwelling for them was essential and the amount of women's communal activity restricted to a minimum. Matters concerning the welfare of the clan were discussed by the males, with the women excluded.

More significant was the attitude that when a wife was brought in from a conquered or friendly trading group she joined her husband's clan and was abandoned by her own. She left her birthplace and her family in spirit as well as in reality. Henceforth she would need all her innate ingenuity

D

and resourcefulness to avoid a status little better than that of her husband's inanimate possessions and animals.

Notes and Bibliography for this chapter are on pp170-2

3 Family Experiments in Early Civilisations

The family was surviving, not as a nuclear unit, but by recognition of the complicated structure of group, clan, or nation. In origin the groupings were based on matriarchy, because the maternal line could always be identified while the paternity of the offspring might be open to doubt, but increased wealth, with the consequent growth of communal power and influence, had shifted control to men. A bride joined her husband's group, sometimes for a price and frequently through capture, instead of remaining a link in her own family line. Thus a wife became an item of masculine property, as were the children she bore. Greed for more wealth and determination to retain it encouraged men of property to seek affiliations with neighbouring groups, their loyalty being most positively assured by arranging marriages so that family kin extended to every allied group. In time the identity of this amalgamation became more important than the nuclear families of which it was composed, and the great family, consisting of three living generations and relatives by blood and marriage in a complicated network of kinship emerged, dominated by one man, whose word was law.

The hybrid nature of this kinship, arbitrarily decided by the chief of the group or a few advisers of the wealthiest and most powerful families in it, was so intricate that cohesion could be maintained only by example backed by the threat of force. The former was encouraged by the emergence of religious and mystical beliefs about the status and destiny of the group, and the latter by legislation. The State, symbolised by palace and temple, was emerging as the organisation controlling the behaviour and prosperity of families, and however deep was the desire of the ruling body to maintain the cultural pattern established by the ancestral family groups a clash of interests was inevitable. One family or group of families gained ascendancy and held its position at the expense of less powerful groups. The existence of more than one or two strong, inward-looking clans within the State was always a potential menace to the ruling class; they had either to be brought into the dominant clan by intimidation or, more conveniently, by union through marriage.

This was perhaps the most formidable assault on the spontaneous family structure mankind had hitherto experienced. For aeons of time change had been so gradual that one generation after another experienced no alteration in the design for living from their ancestors' customs. A young couple expected to imitate the lives of their parents, and their children grew up to do the same. Now old beliefs and customs were being questioned, and often forbidden: a period of change which has been repeated throughout history.

But laws and persuasion could not entirely abolish the emotional and traditional regard for the ties of marriage and kinship. For the subjected and propertyless members of the State the family provided the main refuge from the miseries of servitude and regimentation. For the ruling class the family structure offered a means of guarding and extending wealth and power. All sections of the community were intent on sus-

taining and even elaborating the meaning of family in a nar-
rower sense than the kinship of clan and tribe. Within the
family structure there was an underlying conflict of the sexes.
The politics of power and wealth favoured male domination.
Maternity—and above all the advantageous form of maternity
of a wife whose birthright was membership of a 'good' family
—permitted any resourceful woman, supported by an am-
bitious father, to exert influence on her husband which no
law could entirely eradicate. Thus while an assessment of all
major ancient civilisations, as of modern nations, shows them
to be basically patriarchal, a matriarchal influence has never
entirely disappeared.

The people of the populous communities which formed the
ancient civilisations could identify themselves by their trade
or occupation, by their wealth or lack of it, and by their social
position as governing or governed. The position of the individual in the community was recognised by what he did
rather than by his relationship to others. Yet his family background was really the source of his good or bad fortune.
Property, political power, trade and profession could be inherited. To move out of the category which the family background bestowed at birth demanded exceptional abilities, and
only for excessive disloyalty and misbehaviour could a man be
expelled from it.

Those civilisations which, through the heritage of religion
or political ideology, have stamped their customs of family
and State on the modern West, went through developments
where primitive traditions of family were adapted, moulded,
and frequently corrupted as the State grew in wealth and
power. Their histories reflect the aforementioned hostility of
the State to the family *per se*, and the tenacious, obstinate
determination of the nuclear family to survive.

Sometimes a State's rulers exploited this basic human desire
for family life in its simplest form in order to curb potentially
dangerous forces embodied in the larger male-dominated
family groups. Thanks to the tens of thousands of clay tab-

lets and the State's practice of keeping a chronicle of the principal events of every year, Babylon is a well recorded ancient empire, and can be regarded as typical of the old civilisations of the Middle East. It was formed through conquest and amalgamation of the farmer-warrior tribes dwelling in the fertile plains watered by the Euphrates and the lower Tigris. The great unifier of the city states, with their rigid rules of kinship, marriage and patriarchal control of the family, was Hammurabi, the first dynasty king who reigned for a period estimated to have been in the seventeenth century BC.

In order to unite the mixed races of Sumerians and Semites Hammurabi promulgated a code of laws, some of which were designed to weaken the supremacy of the husband's family, and thus break down the insularity of his group, by conferring generous privileges on women. A wife's dowry had to be held in trust on her behalf by her husband. If he divorced her or he pre-deceased her she was given possession of goods and money to the equivalent value of the dowry. If he took further wives the first wife could sue for compensation. She could engage in trade, buy and sell property, and go to law over commercial disputes. If she were unmarried she could become a priest or a scribe, ie a State official.

Egyptian women were among the most privileged of the early civilisations of the Middle East. The patriarchal system of rule was not so strong as in many other States and Empires of the pre-Christian era. In Egypt's religion the goddess Isis was more powerful than the god Osiris. Women could aspire to official positions in government, and socially they were as free as men. As a result of this respect for women the Egyptian attitude to family life was delightful. A motive for this happy tolerance and high regard for women was in the method of farming. Cultivation of the land bordering the Nile depended on coping with the annual floods. It was anti-social—and impractical—to attempt to erect dams and control irrigation on an acre or so of land without any regard for one's neighbours. Either by agreement or after battle, the harnessing of the water became a co-operative activity, as did the actual cultivation of the fields, the harvesting and storage of the crops, and their protection against marauders. In this stride towards a vast State organisation of the Upper and Lower Nile, based on urban communities, the nuclear family flourished in a degree of freedom unknown since land had become valuable as personal property.

While the emergence of a complex type of agriculture and merchandising meant the creation of numerous social classes, with a directing power at the top, the family pattern was much the same throughout the nation. Egyptian tombs and papyri inevitably commemorate only the lives of kings, warriors and priests, but one can safely assume that their attitude to family life also applied to their subjects. Genuine affection for marriage partner and children was encouraged. The nuclear family typified the ideal of Egyptian life, and was exemplified in the statues and tombs of the ruling families, as early as the third millenium BC, when mother, or wife, or children were commemorated as devotedly as menfolk.

A vivid contrast to this sophisticated culture is seen in the primitive and impoverished tribes of Jews which struggled for existence alongside Egypt and the other great empires of the Middle East. The Hebrews' attitude to social life, surrounding it with an aura of religion which has always proved an effective way of maintaining the *status quo* in marriage and family relationships, was very typical of an agricultural community constantly beset by danger from more powerful neighbours and by the difficulties of finding fertile land in adequate quantity. From the tribal beliefs developed the universal religion of the modern West. It is of interest to note that the original Hebrew concept had little regard for family property and status being maintained from generation to generation, with its accompanying veneration of the ancestral founders of the line. 'Therefore shall a man leave his father and mother, and shall cleave unto his wife: and they shall be one flesh' was the early family policy.[1] The isolation and independence of each new family were not modified to suit the patriarchal system until comparatively late in Hebrew history, the commandment to honour (ie respect and care for) a father and mother eventually being repeated by Jesus and thereafter, of course, regarded as an essential for God-fearing men and women of Christendom.

Once the Jewish tribes had gained cohesion and identity, the maintenance of the family structure, not least in order to increase population, became a strongly enforced custom, although some of their social concepts were in time modelled on those of the Egyptians, their powerful neighbour with enviable prosperity and stability. Family life was idealised to the extent that failure to marry was regarded as sinful for any man. While Jewish religious ritual in public was a male monopoly, within the home the wife was prominent in arranging the religious observances which were concerned with virtually every activity of daily existence. As the bearer of children the Jewish wife earned respect, typified in the prophecy that one day a Jewish woman would be the mother of the Messiah.

But the Jewish family in time became the tool of a male-dominated society, with ambitions to own, increase, and hand on property through the male line. With such an attitude the Jewish wife was, politically, a second-rate citizen. Any man could have four wives if he could afford them, and if a wife committed the unforgivable sin of being barren it was almost inevitable that her husband brought another woman into the family home, however poor he might be. The husband's property interests in his wife were strongly protected by the imposition of swingeing punishment for a wife's sexual infidelity, and to indicate her inferiority she was for a large part of her existence regarded as unclean and unapproachable.

The development of the Jewish family, with the father-husband the sole arbiter of its existence and activities, followed that of the majority of primitive people. Settlement in communities and the adoption of agriculture began, as usual, with communal ownership of land and sharing of labour on it but developed into division of fields owned personally by each family. The vineyard which roused the greed of Ahab could not be handed over by Naboth because 'divine law' forbade the gift of an inheritance to someone else. Property was the means by which a Jewish family was identified. Originally the land and goods were bequeathed to all the sons to be shared out, with the eldest son getting the most or the best. The closest next of kin of the dead man was expected to care for the widow and the orphaned children too young to look after themselves. If the deceased had a brother he was expected to marry the widow and father a son by her, who was then given the father's name.

The monotheism of the Jews supported the concept of male domination just as polytheism, with deities of both sexes, ensured that their powerful neighbours never entirely abandoned the respect and veneration of women, despite the eventual pressure of politics and economics. As the State became more powerful and a highly developed civilisation had to exert fuller control over its subjects for the general good quite as much as for the ruling clique, the family structure was forced to endure more and more interference in its traditions and culture, though memories of the past helped to keep the old customs alive.

The Homeric poems record that the Athenian city state was the result of the characteristic amalgamation of families into clans. Theseus, the legendary hero of Attica, represented in his birth the union of two powerful clans. His father was king of Athens and his mother a daughter of the king of Troezen. The importance of the maternal line in this primitive society was, incidentally, indicated by the fact that the boy was brought up in his mother's clan, and only on reaching maturity did his father recognise him as his heir. Underlying the romantic and martial adventures of Theseus was the story of the union of the peoples of Attica. There were four principal tribes, each consisting of three groups of kinsfolk, with each of these groups formed from thirty families. Theseus became the head of between three and four hundred of the most important families scattered through twelve urban centres and their adjacent territories. He made Athens the centre of government and, in the manner of all political leaders, set about weakening the nuclear family. He ignored the ancient ties of blood and marriage, created a class system consisting of an aristocracy of warriors and political leaders, a middle class of peasant farmers, and a working class of artisans and servants. As a result the aristocracy severed its links with families and kinsfolk, both as regards personal control of the younger members' marriages and physically in the sense that its members no longer lived on the ancestral lands but enjoyed the revenues from them while residing in Athens. In order to maintain the monopoly of wealth and power the upper class arranged marriages within their class, irrespective of the ancestral origins of family, clan, and, when wars were not in progress, of tribe as well. In this policy of strengthening the Establishment men were the arbiters of marriage arrangements.

Despite the nationalistic policies of the emerging State, it was, as always, impossible entirely to erase family loyalties and replace them with unalloyed patriotism except perhaps at tribal level, and then only by ruthless discipline. The nadir of human relationship was achieved in Sparta, ruled by a warrior caste of some 30,000 men at the height of its power, holding about 600,000 Helots and Perioechi in slavery and servitude. The State maintained its supremacy over other groups in Attica and during wars against the Persians and Thebans by restricting the family life of the ruling caste with laws awesome in their effectiveness for the intended purpose: the breeding of warriors. The sole object of marriage was to produce healthy male children. Girls who had been reprieved from death in infancy were subjected to rigorous exercises designed to develop their physical strength and pugnacity. At the age of eighteen they were judged to be at the peak of sexual fertility and physical prowess, and ready for maternity. The husbands selected for them, who were given ceaseless military training from the age of seven, continued to live in military camps and were permitted to visit their wives only during the hours of darkness. For their cultural and emotional satisfaction Spartan warriors were encouraged to make homosexual alliances with their superiors in rank in the army. A married woman could take an approved lover and the child born of the affair was regarded as that of her official husband. A Spartan mother who bore sickly sons, or too many daughters, willingly exposed them outside the town to die or to be eaten by predatory animals. She was ready to stab to death any son who was proved a coward.

The efficiency of the Spartan culture undoubtedly produced a physically splendid people. Their methods of infant feeding and child care were enlightened, and the preoccupation with health throughout life was far in advance of any of their contemporaries. It would be satisfying to believe the virtual abolition of family life in any shape or form carried the seeds of destruction of Sparta. But the disturbing truth is that Sparta flourished from her origin as a small centre of civilisation in the second millenium BC and her power did not permanently decline until, with the rest of Greece, she submitted to Rome in 221 BC. A nation of considerable size thus succeeded in erasing most of the emotional influences inherent in family life for more than a thousand years.

Fortunately, no other nation bequeathing ideas to the modern world has ever seriously attempted to emulate Sparta's system. The insane experiments of the Nazi regime as regards selective breeding of a ruling caste of desirable Aryans were of a minor and, luckily, temporary nature. It is fortunate that the race theorists of Hitlerite Germany were so bemused by Teutonic mysticism that the practical and efficient methods of Sparta were ignored.

Mankind has usually had a higher regard for the loftier policies inaugurated by the peoples who were Sparta's uneasy neighbours. The genius springing from the people who lived in Athens offered new ideas which transformed politics, science, and philosophy. Perhaps the same awareness of human needs and capabilities was the reason why the family structure obstinately managed to retain its ancient customs and conventions, the changes which occurred being the inevitable developments of advances in wealth and civilisation.

The head of an Athenian family, who was sometimes old enough to be father, grandfather and great grandfather, was the arbiter of every member's destiny, and his word was rarely questioned. This power was supported by the acceptance that he was also a priest, in communication with the ancestral gods. The religious tinge of family life permeated most of the tribes which comprised the Athenian nation. At the time Solon formulated his laws (circa 593 BC) religious brotherhoods, three in each tribe, and each composed of the heads of families who could trace a common ancestry, directed the lives of every man, woman, child, and slave. Long before the Athenian nation had gained a cohesive identity the religious brotherhoods had established a system of private ownership of land and property within each family, and the family heads had the right to prevent any land being transferred by sale or marriage from the family's possession.

Democracy developing in the City State influenced the decline of this arbitrary system of family kinship dominating everyone's life. The artists and craftsmen, the peasants, and the merchants gradually gained a social status of their own, at some cost to the privileges of the old brotherhoods and tribal groups. But the legislation of Solon, classifying people according to their landed property (and ignoring other sources of wealth or reasons for prestige), ensured that the ruling classes were forced to regard marriage as an arrangement to protect family interests. Men of property therefore bequeathed their lands and possessions to the eldest son. If a man had no son his daughter was encouraged to marry her father's closest male relative, who then became the next of kin, thereby ensuring the continuance of the line exclusively through the paternal family. With the prestige and civic privileges of a family dependent on property, marriage was naturally regarded as a momentous step.

Until inter-family negotiations had arranged her marriage an Athenian girl was completely subject to the control of her father, or if he were absent or dead, to the eldest brother or a paternal uncle. She was confined to the women's section of the house if her family was wealthy enough to possess more than one room. Her relaxation was to play and walk in the inner courtyard of her home. The segregation of the sexes until marriage, and the deliberate avoidance of a passionate union after it, encouraged sexual inversion. Though neither male homosexuality nor lesbianism were new aberrations of the human psyche, the Athenians made both into a cult and, in the case of male homosexuality, a virtue. This may not be so much indicative of moral decadence as of precautions against uncontrolled emotions having the result of producing offspring which would not be acceptable in the family structure.

The subservience of women in the male-dominated organisation of family life was too strongly entrenched—and too valuable to those in the oligarchy—to be changed. Yet the Athenian idealism of human personality could not exclude women: a well-born girl received some education and was taught to be proud of her social status, both as an individual and as a member of an illustrious family. But when she grew up and married she found she had no place in the social and civic life of Athens. Women were rarely seen in the streets, even if accompanied by a husband. Female slaves were expected to complete the household shopping in the early morning and be back inside their masters' houses before the day's activities filled the streets and squares with men. However, a wife of a wealthy and distinguished family might retain considerable independence of action, and a bride realised that her private and personal life could be much as she wished it. As a result marriage among the elite was a soulless affair, each partner seeking a worry-free and independent existence.

Sexual attraction was regarded as unimportant. In the words of Demosthenes, Athenians 'marry a woman in order to beget legitimate children and to have a faithful guardian of the household; [they] keep concubines for service and daily care, and *hetairi* for the enjoyment of love'.

The wealthy wife brought a dowry with her, but it remained an insurance for her future. Divorce was easily obtained, usually on equal terms for both men and women. A wife who was divorced was entitled to receive back her dowry. This dowry was also a form of guarantee that she was in effect paying to enjoy the privileges of marriage and motherhood. If her husband proved impotent or infertile, then a wife's deliberately planned coitus with another man (preferably a blood relation of her husband) for the purpose of conception was condoned, even though adultery solely for amorous reasons could bring severe punishment.

The customs on the birth of a child symbolised the importance of the father and the subservience of the mother. A husband was not expected to see his wife once labour had begun, nor for some days afterwards. A female slave trained in midwifery tended the mother and then brought the child to the father. He examined it, noted its sex and looked for signs of ill health or malformation. He then announced his decision on whether the child should be nursed or exposed to die. The forebodings of Athenian wives who knew that their husbands did not wish for more offspring were a reason for the prevalence of abortions during the first month or so of pregnancy, termination of pregnancy being acceptable at any time before the embryo 'quickened'.

It is hardly surprising that, with marriage so frequently a business arrangement and co-habitation a boring duty, Athens delighted in the vicarious experience of plays and stories. Their gods and goddesses were amorous and violent, though almost always there was the moral that unrestrained passions brought tragedy in their train and that the path of requited love rarely ended in lasting joy. The lesson was that the family's welfare transcended the happiness of the individual, if that happiness was derived from sexual interest.

The typical male member of a leading Athenian family put off marriage as long as he could. With the onset of middle age, and perhaps on the death of his father, he accepted that an official heir was urgently required. Age differences between the selected bride and himself weakened the feeling of comradeship, and her sexual attractiveness could actually be a disadvantage. Athenian men were not enthusiastic about fathering large families. The birth of a male heir or two was the purpose of the marriage; daughters were just burdens who would need dowries in due course.

By the time an Athenian married he was sophisticated and probably satiated with sexual experiences. Athens established houses of prostitution as part of civic life, an exclusive enterprise of the State and situated in special zones. The women were not permitted to leave the area and had to wear a designated style of dress. The Athenian prostitute was the only woman with whom an unmarried man could freely associate, and over the years she earned social importance for herself. The luxury and wealth an Athenian prostitute could enjoy attracted foreign women, to whom the laws and customs restricting the freedom of Athenian women did not apply. These beautiful and talented girls, the *hetairai*, might become partners in a secondary family unit, especially if they bore children. Their companionship was as socially acceptable as it was sexually satisfying. *Hetairai* joined the schools of such philosophers as Socrates, Plato and Aristotle. Whatever progress was made in Athens for the real emancipation of woman, the *hetairai* were largely responsible. Many abandoned commercialised sex, and offered only intellectual companionship to their clients. A rich Athenian could have in effect two households—that of his burdensome wife and family and the pleasant residence of his hetaira.

The acknowledged contempt for conventional family life eventually spelt the doom of Athens. In a world where manpower was vital for survival the decline in population made her a treasure quite easily captured by the Romans. In the fourth century BC Athens could call on 27,000 adult male citizens to defend the City State. Despite interminable wars this number remained fairly constant for more than a century. Then the decline set in. Polybius, writing in the second century BC, claimed the cities were empty and the land uncultivated because men 'would no longer marry, or if they did, would raise one, or at the most two, children'. The independence and influence of the nuclear family had been effectively curbed; as it faded the State declined as well.

Across the sea a fecund people, the Romans, were able to overwhelm Attica by sheer weight of numbers. The Roman nation originated from the typical amalgamation of groups of farming families, inter-marrying in order to increase the population and area of cultivated land, and gradually amalgamating into tribes. The unity of the groups was encouraged by the menace of the numerous hostile tribes around them, and the farmers developed the arts of war in order to protect, and later expand, their territory. The Roman family system was patrician, and until laws were codified in the fifth century BC all decisions were made by the senior male of the family, the responsibility being handed down from father to son. The word *familia* described membership of a large household, presided over by the oldest married man, and embraced every living person, including slaves. It was not a term restricted to relatives by marriage and birth.

This paternal domination was concerned with the status and reputation of the large family, its ancestors, and its future descendants. It did not trespass on the prestige and veneration accorded to that formidable and splendid woman, the Roman matron. The wife of an absent warrior enjoyed high status, and the men of her clan regarded it as a dishonour to themselves, quite as much to the absent husband if that status was besmirched.

The moral code of the early Romans demanded suicide by

a wife who was unfaithful while her husband was absent at the wars. This was not so much because of the sin of breaking her marriage vows but to avoid the possible birth of a child which could not be accepted as a pure-bred member of the family. The attitude to self-inflicted death prevailed throughout the life of the Roman Empire. The idea of killing oneself because of personal unhappiness was absurd in a Roman's eyes: the tragedy was personal and did not affect the family, the clan, or the State. Only a human action or a twist of Fate damaging the honour of the family name merited solution by suicide. Anyone who lacked the courage to destroy himself risked assassination by relatives—and few would criticise such an execution under the written or unwritten law.

This fierce loyalty to the family remained dominant, although it developed naturally into loyalty to Rome above all else. Conquerors of most of the known world, the Romans remained members of the tribe of Latins who founded the Empire, and their loyalty was to the family structure of those early farmer-warriors. The Latins created a City State which at first was administered by *curiae*, representing the old identity of the tribes, and composed of the heads of families. In time the city became more important than the families which had created it, and the family chiefs lost their influence. The efforts of the plebeians, immigrants from other tribes, and junior members of the families only distantly related to the direct male line, to enjoy civic and political privileges, brought about a form of democracy and a republican regime. Kinship and the rights of rule through family prestige were extended to embrace new members, not without resentment by the old guard.

Thus the pattern of marriage and family life in Rome followed that of most peoples progressing from a loosely affiliated group of peasants to a property-owning civilisation. The most ancient form of marriage was later given the name of *coemptio*, which involved mutual purchase, the groom buying his wife from her family and she bringing a dowry given by

E

her parents. Later this ceremony became an exchange of gifts directly between bride and groom. Long after Rome became a major power this form of marriage prevailed for the plebeian classes, largely because neither of the families had much property, and concern about the family fortunes was minimal.

Among the patrician classes the male line became all-important, and the worth of a bride was chiefly assessed as a source of increased wealth and prestige for the husband's family, to the extent that in a marriage where one or both of the marriage partners had no property to exchange or share, the union was not socially recognised, and could easily be annulled by law. In such a case the wife might safeguard herself as a married woman by *usus*, a sort of common law marriage necessitating evidence that she had lived with a man for a year and had not left him for more than three consecutive nights. Proof of this co-habitation, of course, could be satisfactory only if the husband confirmed it. In a marriage instituted by *coemptio* or recognised as *usus* the ruling class did not automatically recognise the children as lawful beneficiaries of the father or the father's family. The children were regarded as fatherless and they took their mother's family name. The socially acceptable marriage was *matrimonium justum*, in which the husband had complete authority over his bride and exclusive possession of her dowry, her father formally ceding his authority over his daughter at the wedding.

As early as 450 BC the Roman husband had legal provisions as regards his rights and duties. He could kill a child who was deformed or monstrous. He had the right during the lifetime of his children (apparently into adult life, or until they married) to scourge, put in chains, set to manual labour, or imprison them. His main responsibility was to educate and support his children. No illegitimate child had any claim on his father. Romans exulted in their reputation for firmness and courage, two of their seven virtues. But these characteristics did not, within the family, banish sentiment and tolerance. Despite the law permitting destruction of malformed babies comparatively few instances are recorded, and infanticide on these grounds was not as prevalent as it had been in Greece.

The formal introduction of the child to the family took place eight or nine days after its birth, when its life was reasonably assured. Both mother and father were present, along with any other children of the marriage and relatives of both parents. The father showed his acknowledgement of the child as his by lifting it in his arms and pronouncing its name. Even in the largest households, in times of peace, parents and children were constantly together because family life was centred in the *atrium*, where stood waxen or sculpted masks of paternal ancestors and the shrines of the Lares and Penates, the guardians of the field and household, typifying the ancient veneration of family life. Until the age of seven the children were constantly with their mother. Then the sons were permitted to accompany their father on his daily activities, while the daughters began to learn womanly tasks in the home.

This simple and affectionate type of family life declined with the social upheaval during civil wars, but even more with the general increase in wealth and the reliance on slave labour to shoulder almost every activity in daily life. Slaves took over the care of children from the day of their birth. The responsibility of the father to teach his sons literacy and arithmetic lapsed when State schools provided education in the first century BC. The mother's traditional duty of educating daughters in spinning, weaving, and housewifery was transferred to a household slave, if such mundane tasks were considered worth teaching at all.

After the Punic wars (which finally ended in 146 BC) Rome's prosperity increased enormously. Proud and wealthy families jealously protected their assets, among which their daughters' marriage prospects could be turned to the family's advantage. While occasionally there might be advantages in arranging the marriage of a daughter into a family of greater distinction than her own, generally speaking the paterfamilias was quite content to devote his energies and scheming to the progress of his own family, and had little desire to marry off his daughter by offering her with a large dowry. Marriage in Rome began, almost accidentally, to develop into the modern style, with a man and girl feeling mutually attracted, and a decreasing degree of control by the parents of either partner, though, of course, laws about marriage across the classes applied, and the romance had to be between socially (and politically) suitable persons.

These 'romantic' marriages were less successful than arranged unions. Divorce became easy for anyone with wealth and political influence, the only penalty being a financial one. The guilty husband had to hand over assets equal to the value of the dowry, and a guilty wife lost part of it on divorce, despite the fact that legally it was still her family's property. This was a far cry from the ancient law which allowed a husband to kill his wife if he found her actually committing adultery, while a wronged wife was forbidden even to slap her erring husband.

Neither the increasing power of the State nor legislation could wholly destroy the traditional respect for the Roman wife. Though legally completely subjected to her husband ('marital rights' of a husband was a Roman idea) she tenaciously held on to her ancient role as the architect of the family fortunes. Constant warfare continued to mean that for long periods a wife was in sole charge of household, farm or workshop, allocating tasks, punishing offenders, and rearing offspring. As Rome's domination was extended over most of Italy and then through Europe and the Near East these military expeditions could leave the Roman wife in sole charge for months and even years. The civil administrators who followed the expeditionary armies might expect to remain in the colonies for half a lifetime. Some took their families with them, but the Roman respect for the ancestral estates could mean that such a permanent removal was impractical. Some wives who found themselves in a position of absolute control of their households, with no one to criticise or advise,

equipped themselves with knowledge to shoulder these masculine responsibilities. Many, however, regarded the situation
as one of freedom from male dominance. Slaves could be put
in charge of the household while their employer pursued
pleasure and amusement.

In the closing years of the slowly dying Roman Empire, the
deterioration in family life, with its accompanying laxness of
morals and excesses of luxurious living, provided rich evidence for ascetic Christians in pointing to the disastrous results
of a decline in moral and social standards, an attitude which
has persisted until today. Whether Rome died because of its
enthusiasm for a mode of life which by most standards was
decadent or for deeper economic and strategic reasons is an
arguable point. But long before Rome fell much of the ancient
stability and most of the honourable aims of the family were
almost dead. Marriage itself became unfashionable despite
attempts to restore family life by offering grants for childbirth, penalties for failure to marry, and heavy fines for the
guilty party in a divorce. None of these State efforts was of
much avail. A superbly organised government machine, controlled by men so highly regarded that they frequently earned
the title of divine beings, had sometimes involuntarily, but
always for reasons of State, eroded the stability and constancy
of the pattern of family life which had made the growth of a
world empire possible. The crumbling of the fabric composed
of family units made the eventual collapse of the whole
Roman edifice inevitable. The ruins were past restoration.
The concept of the family could be rebuilt—on the principles
of a Judaic-Christian culture. For centuries to come the
State's interference in family life was to be restricted and
moulded by the tradition of religious belief.

Note and Bibliography for this chapter are on pp172-3

4 *The Christian Compromise*

The decline of Rome's political and military power was so gradual that a complete breakdown on a world-wide scale of Roman cultural and social practices did not occur in the lifetime of a particular generation. It was a period of comparatively gradual change, with features of the old order surviving among the new, both affected by the traditional cultures of pre-Roman tribes and clans. During the three centuries of the Empire's decline large numbers of people in well-governed areas—of which the occupied part of Britain was one—had been so thoroughly disciplined that the Roman-style family structure could withstand the breakdown in communication with Rome and the deterioration in governmental control, so far as the communities in the garrison towns and along the military roads were concerned.

Outside these fairly localised districts the age-old pattern of pagan European family life had never been greatly changed: tribal customs based on kinship in an agricultural community and practices conforming to religious belief in an Earth Mother survived.

The family pattern of the Germanic tribes who spread throughout Western Europe had two forms. First there was the household of parents and children; secondly the great family of kin, membership of which was traced through both father and mother: hence children could claim kinship with two groups. This great family (*moegth* in Anglo-Saxon Britain and *sippe* among the Frisians) controlled the behaviour of the households of which it was composed, overriding the dominance of the father as regards the welfare of his children while the mother was protected by the fact that she remained a member of her own kinship. A wife of resolution, enjoying the prestige of a powerful kin, retained a considerable degree of independence. Wives of chiefs often enjoyed authority comparable to that of their husbands, particularly during the latter's frequent absences in war and on expeditions to discover new territory for settlement. The attitude that a chief's wife was a potential ruler is typified in the crowning of the consort at a king's coronation or, if already a king, on his marriage.

Ethelwulf inaugurated the formal procedure of crowning a king's consort on his marriage in 856. Since that time every English king has made his wife a queen (and therefore co-monarch)—a tradition which was a cause of misgivings before the abdication of Edward VIII. Tribal queens could prove as formidable adversaries as tribal kings. Boadicea ruled the Iceni tribe in the northern part of East Anglia after her husband died.[1] When the whole tribe was insulted by Rome's action in having the queen flogged and her two daughters raped every fit man took up arms to wreak revenge.

The Romans, obstinately convinced that by destroying the paternalistic strength of a family they could effectively break kinship loyalties, concentrated on killing off fit men, enslaving them or moving them to fight as mercenaries in another part of the Empire. But tribal loyalty to the ruling family could survive so long as a daughter existed to carry on the family line. Wiser Romans in control of local areas came to understand this fact, and pacification was made easier by a Roman administrator, or a member of his family, marrying a woman belonging to a powerful British family than by capturing her father or brothers.

The waves of invaders—Angles, Saxons, and Vikings—who later swept into the western European lands of the Roman Empire shared, of course, traditions about a woman's status in the family and clan or tribe. The spearheads of invasion were composed of young men travelling without their womenfolk. Intermarriage between invader and conquered was inevitable, and in the event an acceptable method of demonstrating the end of hostilities. Both the Angles and the Saxons practised bride purchase. A wife was a piece of property with a defined value. The price paid for a bride went to her father, or if he were dead to the male relative appointed as the protector of the unwed women of the family. Where no blood relative existed the chief of the clan, as titular head of all the families, took the responsibility for the welfare of single women and received the bride price for them. The sexual benefits which a bride conferred were not entirely ignored. A Saxon custom was for the groom to present his wife with a present (*morgaengife*) on the morning after the wedding night, which she displayed as proof of the consummation of marriage. For reasons of prestige a man would make this gift as valuable as he could afford. Athelstan, first king of a united England, extracted the city of Magdrberg as the gift of his sister's bridegroom, Otto of Germany.

The Anglo-Saxon groups had a strong sense of community. Just as land was held in common for every family, so were the members of the family common owners of the house and its equipment. A family was identified as consisting of the occupants of a house, and as households grew larger and more complex embraced other relatives than grandparents, parents, and children. The death of the oldest male did not automatically end the family's position in the community. The share of work and land continued on the same basis until a surviving son was old enough to be its representative, leader, and adviser. A noteworthy exception to the general sharing was that the actual home was customarily handed to the youngest son. There was a practical reason for this. In the normal span of a father's life older sons would have reached adulthood and married before his death, having their own households. The youngest son would often be a mere child still dependent on his mother. By inheriting the home his mother's future as well as the child's were secure.

The arrival of Christianity in Britain had little effect on these customs for generation after generation. The Norse invasions were in an area of the country never really Christian; under Danish occupation the Danelaw area reverted to paganism. So far as the people's social life was concerned, the new Eastern religion, with its overtones of Roman culture, sought to impose beliefs about marriage and family life which must have been utterly bewildering to a people whose aims included as many children as possible and the development of the family as a powerful and wealthy unit. The early Christian missionaries were steeped in the understandable belief that pagan Rome, with all she stood for, was the arch enemy of Christianity. The moral degeneracy of Rome appeared to go hand in hand with attempted suppression of the new religion. Condemnation of any regard for sexual pleasure seemed to be essential if the ascetic ideals of Christianity were ever to be turned into reality in men's lives. Absolute chastity was held up as an ideal. That this way of life, if completely successful, would have destroyed the family and brought about a decrease and eventual end of humanity was not so ridiculous as it may now appear: the end of the world was regarded as imminent. Compromise was necessary in the light of experience. The most zealous missionary had to accept that the majority of people, born with original sin in their beings, wanted to marry. For a couple to wed without a vestige of mutual desire was a perfectly acceptable idea of people who rarely married for any reason except in obedience to their parents or for material gain. What was new was the inculcation that the sexual pleasures which followed marriage were reprehensible. Intercourse, people were told, was to be regarded as tolerable for one purpose only: the procreation of offspring. For some four centuries after Britain's conversion to Christianity a religious wedding ceremony was not regarded as necessary for the establishment of a legal union and the legitimisation of children. At best the couple might stand in the porch or within the holy ground on which the church stood and exchange vows. Later, in order to restrict promiscuity, abolish polygamy and curb the incidence of divorce, the Church developed a religious ceremony at which a priest officiated, and thereby could direct the subsequent behaviour of the married couple.

This religious control had the effect of turning married life into something of a penance. Intercourse was sinful during the hours of daylight; after the first meal of the day and before the last one; on Sundays, Holy Days, during Lent, during pregnancy and for a specified number of days after childbirth; the night before and the night after attending Mass; and the hour before and the hours after praying or reading the Bible. A devout couple, attending Mass daily, had very few occasions when sexual intercourse was permissible.

This attitude to sex, even within marriage, resulted in numerous forms of aberration and perversion in neurotic attempts to sublimate natural appetites. They ranged from the extremes of self-castration and flagellation to the repressions of unconsummated courtly love, and in the more reasonable solution of entering an enclosed order where chastity was at least made easier. Whatever the psychological harm to the individual the social damage lay in the dismissal of the wife-mother from her prior position of respect and regard. This had the paradoxical result of enhancing the status of the husband-father to a position in the family much the same as he had held in the Roman culture which Christianity was intended to erase. It did so, not by lauding the virtues of fatherhood and family, but by denigrating women to a level below that of animals.

'It is good for a man not to touch a woman';[2] 'it is better to marry than to burn',[3] and similar Pauline aspersions against women supported the legend of Eve tempting Adam and therefore her disgrace as the source of sin. Women were degraded to such an extent that bishops assembling at Macon in AD 585 could solemnly discuss whether women were human. In the thirteenth century misogynists derived some satisfaction from the theory of St Thomas Aquinas that woman's inferiority was due to some mysterious defect during pre-natal life.

It was very difficult for any man genuinely accepting the authority of the Church to regard his wife with anything but contempt; he had to suppress feelings of admiration for her and joy in her companionship. Her sexual attractions could not be regarded as pleasurable with a clear conscience. Tertullian, in De Virginibus Velandis, explained that woman was the gate of hell, the source of all ills, and should spend her days in perpetual penance for Eve's sin. For a devout woman this condemnation was an almost insupportable burden.[4]

Yet Christianity did confer benefits as regards the welfare of children. Infanticide, accepted by preceding and contemporary societies as a reasonable and even desirable means of having the required size and quality of offspring, became a crime. This was a reversal of the law of the Empire in which the early Christians lived. This was an historic advance in the regard for individual human life, but it did not necessarily strengthen the family or the clan of which the individual was a part. Infanticide was, and among some primitive peoples still is, practised as a means of reducing the effects of severe poverty. Infanticide during the farmer-warrior stage of development killed off surplus female babies as a source of needless expense and of no use as fighters. Among the highly civilised people of the pre-Christian era this tendency to killing female babies persisted for the same reasons but more often infanticide was for the purpose of destroying deformed children.

Abortion was introduced later in human history than infanticide as a means of controlling the size of the family, for the obvious reason that it demanded knowledge of the physiology of conception and birth. The attitude of pre-Christian peoples to it was somewhat different from their opinions on infanticide. Usually it was the idea of the woman, and rarely carried out to the order of her husband or male relatives. Incest, rape, and intercourse with an enemy were justified reasons to insist that a woman, particularly a married one, should submit to induced abortion. But then, as now, it was more frequently the private and secretive action of the woman for what she regarded as her own welfare. The prevalence of induced abortion is a rough measure of the degree of independence of wives, for it infers contact with other women to exchange information and often the direct aid of another woman to help induce abortion. To some extent this secretive co-operation among the women of a group has usually been made easier by midwives in all countries where abortion is a crime or costly.

The Christian Church proclaimed that the destruction of an embryo or a new-born child was a sin, maintaining such a rigid insistence that repulsion about it has for centuries been so ingrained that it is very difficult for the population of any Christian country to understand the attitude of earlier civilisation in regarding abortion and infanticide as acceptable practices.

The Church in time also condemned divorce, an action previously regarded as socially beneficial until it was abused in the general decadence of Rome during her decline. This Christian policy was another step forward in enhancing the stability of the family, and the principal beneficiary was the wife. Divorce has invariably been a feature of male-dominated societies until modern times, and frequently the husband's action to put away his erring wife was the only admissible one.

The spread of organised Christianity created a code of living for everyone, high and low, wealthy or poor, in which doctrine deprecated the sexual appetites which brought men and women together, and demanded that they be suppressed or sublimated. If that proved impossible, as of course for the majority it did, then the cohabitation of a man and woman had to be based on high moral principles. On balance it is clear that the Christian family was an advance on anything which had preceded it, even if the laws which fashioned it were a compromise to blend physical needs with spiritual ideals.

The secular influences of the first millenium of the Christian era on family life emerged as a result of the general breakdown of centralised governments in Europe during the so-called Dark Ages, and with it some weakening of the temporal power of the Church. The old system of inter-family relationships re-emerged as the most resourceful social system of Western Europe. Feudalism was a revival of two ancient Roman customs, first of *patrocinium*, the relationship of families in a clan, by which a freeman enjoyed the protection and support of the clan leader in return for the services of himself and his family; and secondly, the *precarium*, which was the grant of land by the chief to freemen. The grant was in effect a loan, for the tenant had no rights over the land and the owner could retrieve it whenever he wished.

The result of the spread of feudalism in Western Europe was that the mass of the population were peasants, some owning a few acres of land and others living as tenants, and freemen of various categories, but invariably holding property under a tenancy. The unity between lord and vassal was as solemn as in any family link. The vassal indicated his homage by extending his clasped hands for the lord to grasp and at the same time making a vow of loyalty (*fealty*). In return the lord bestowed the benefice of sufficient land (*fief*) to support the vassal and his family. The *fief* gradually became a hereditary benefit. Thus, in the midst of a nationally restive period local groups enjoyed stability as members of a great family, the units not necessarily having a common kinship but bound together by pledges of loyalty and the security of livelihood.

The secular lords and the religious houses owned by far the largest proportion of cultivated land, their manors consisting of huge estates self-sufficient in food, drink, domesticated animals, textiles, weapons and agricultural tools, and of course manpower. The harder work was carried out by serfs and villeins bound to the manor and in practice having few privileges much different from the slaves who had worked the estates of Greece and Rome. But one important advance was their right to marry and enjoy family life, however poor and miserable their living conditions might be. As movement beyond the boundaries of the manorial lands was restricted, inter-marriage was customary, and a close-knit community emerged, notable for its class system. Serfs and villeins could not hope to marry into the families of freemen, nor freemen into the vassal and lord groups, though propinquity inevitably resulted in some offspring being hybrids of two classes. The father in a social class superior to that of the mother would not deign to acknowledge her child as his; a man fathering a child on a woman of a superior class would not dare to do so. Consequently most children of the feudal ages, whether born in wedlock or base born, enjoyed the social status of their mothers.

The stable, close-knit family under feudalism was vital for prosperity, with the result that marriage was a carefully considered business arrangement, a woman's desirability as a wife being assessed on the value of her dowry and the economic and social benefits which a union with her family would bring. The valuable property in the dowry was invariably land, and as the value of land decreases if it is divided only one or two daughters could expect to have land as part of a dowry and therefore be marriageable. The eldest son inherited the major estates. Younger sons, and possibly a daughter or two, might get small manors or pieces of less valuable property. Less fortunate sons could move to the towns and become merchants or craftsmen, fight as mercenary soldiers in other countries, or join the priesthood. Unmarried daughters had the choice of a religious life as a vocaton or mundane tasks in the household of a male relative—the role of the spinster, now often a term of tolerant pity rather than the description of a craftswoman.

In England the Norman invasion resulted in a rigidly enforced form of feudalism, which included compulsory primogeniture. By its enforcement the monarch ensured that the feudal lands which were in his gift could only be inherited intact. The Norman family holding the *fief* was eager enough to preserve the existing order in an occupied and defeated country, and as the estate passed intact from one eldest son to the next these families became powerful and wealthy. By devising the idea of an entailed estate, with each family head holding the land in trust for his descendants, the feudal lords effectively prevented the monarch from confiscating the lands for some genuine or trumped up political treason such as treason or disloyalty.

The majority of the noble families could be relied on to remain loyal to the Crown because it was to their advantage to protect the throne and the *status quo*. But with the growth of the influence of Parliament monarch and feudal lords became rivals, and under Henry VIII permanent entails were virtually ended. Long before this death blow to feudalism a new form of social structure had been developing both in England and Europe. The junior members of the manorial families who moved into the growing towns had perforce to be enterprising and independent in outlook, and mediaeval England saw the start of urban industries in many towns each with a population of a few thousand, a development originating in twelfth century Italy and the towns along the Rhine. This mercantile class created a form of family life different from that of a feudal society. Marriages could be spontaneous actions by the two persons concerned, forming a genuine partnership. Industries were carried on in the home. The man was the master craftsman and his wife was his working partner, rather than lackey. In many crafts, such as weaving, knitting, spinning, baking and brewing, the wife did most of the work, and on her skill and output the family prosperity depended quite as much as on the husband's ability to sell the products profitably. Consequently the town-dwelling wife began to enjoy prestige and a degree of independence unknown to her rural sister. She was a member of what in time was called the bourgeoisie, a social class largely free from the restrictions and privileges of heredity and creating its own customs, conventions, and taboos.

Urbanisation, and the activities of industry and commerce which it fostered, paved the way for the Renaissance. Wealthy mercantile families, seeking for their own culture, looked back to the glories of Athens and Rome. Along with their sponsorship of art and literature, these families adopted more liberal customs of sexual behaviour and strengthened their political and social status by devising their own codes for suitable marriages—usually cynical assessments of the commercial advantages accruing. The Church's influence on marriage and the family was directly attacked because of the political advantages that might accrue from an assault. The Reformation made marriage a civil contract as well as, or instead of, a religious institution. The clergy could marry; divorce was possible, and re-marriage after it; the monarch, and not the Pope, was the arbiter of people's lives.

The family was being forced into the centre of the political arena. Its pattern was soon to be manipulated for reasons of national power and prestige rather than for the welfare of its individual members.

Notes and Bibliography for this chapter are on pp173-4

5 *The Changing Role of the Family*

The Reformation was a shattering revolution in the history of organised Christianity and all that it meant as regards social life. The first missionaries had converted emperors, kings, and chieftains, with the assurance that their subjects would follow their leaders' example. Those of the Reformation preached to the ordinary people, so the new sects were at first localised, their beliefs disseminated among members of their family and their neighbours. Religious belief became a decisive factor in marriage arrangements. Persons wanting to marry had to be of the same sect, or one partner (usually the woman) had to agree to change belief and join the dominant religious group. For the underprivileged, and for those who had no reason to attempt to uphold the old order of things on the grounds of great wealth and distinguished lineage, personal attributes were becoming a consideration in the suitability of a marriage partner. Similarity of religious practice, mental outlook, and emotional feelings were ingredients of genuinely mutual affection, arising without considerations of material assets. The love match became an acceptable type of marriage, socially advantageous because it could strengthen the struggling, and often persecuted, religious sect to which the couple's families

F

belonged.

In England a Protestant king holding the dominant place as defender of the official religion of the nation, instead of a Pope in a foreign country, created a conscious awareness of national unity. The legislative procedures which controlled an Englishman's life were enforced by someone he could know and see but who was nevertheless representative of the divinely approved monarch. The Tudor parish constable was responsible for civil administration. It was he who enforced the nationally approved secular laws and organised social welfare, working in co-operation, as regards the observance of the moral and religious laws, with the churchwarden.

Twice a year the churchwarden made a report on sexual offences, drunkenness, and infringement of religious laws such as failure to attend church, ribald behaviour in the churchyard or church, and eating meat on fast days. As always occurs when morality and good behaviour become a State responsibility, this church official devoted most of his time to investigating sexual offences. If adultery was proved, the culprits were publicly condemned and made to do penance for six months. Incest, sexual perversions, and prostitution were punished much more severely. The reputation and security of family was under State protection, and those who jeopardised its security were liable to harsher punishment than under the old regime of the monasteries and manorial lords. Thus in sixteenth century England the State began to impose its control on family life in a manner which has become more strict and all-embracing ever since.

Under Henry VIII the village constable and his assistants had the duty of supervising the day-to-day existence of the mass of people. The workman had the hours of work and his rate of pay imposed by law. All single persons between twelve and sixty years of age who possessed under forty shillings a year had to work as hired servants if required (a regulation which made marriage popular). No employer could dismiss a workman until he had approached the parish constable. An employee wishing to leave his job had to obtain official approval before he was permitted to step across the parish boundaries. People who could not or would not take a job under the official regulations became nomads, hounded from parish to parish. Henry VIII approved the licensing of beggars provided they had some physical or mental disability. Vagabonds were whipped, and in 1557, in the reign of Mary fit persons who begged or wandered homelessly were branded.

Elizabeth I's historic Poor Law Acts of 1597 and 1601 were enlightened social legislation to deal with a crisis of unemployment and inflation, but they replaced the charity of the churches and monasteries of the past with an unsentimental policy of controlling the activities of any family which committed the offence of being poor.[1] The hapless families whose only offence was to have to roam around in search of work were cross-examined and the man's birthplace or last place of permanent residence ascertained, and in 1662 every man, woman and child had to have a settled parish, by birth, apprenticeship, or occupying a house there. Those who could not prove their right to be in a parish were passed from parish to parish on a written itinerary until they arrived at what was regarded as their official home. Once there they had to be given food and shelter, and if the letter of the law was being observed, would be put to work in crafts and manufactures in houses of correction or workhouses, using raw materials the parish was supposed to maintain for the purpose. This was an early version of the modern regimentation by the State in moving people into New Towns from depressed areas and so on.

Villagers, alarmed by the prospect of helping to support local people who had left the district because they could find no work, demanded that their constable should be constantly on the alert for the presence of strangers. He had to admit them if the justices' certificate authorised their arrival. Otherwise the traversing of the parish lands was enforced as fast as possible. Abandoned or deprived children became social outcasts for life. The parish sent them away, as soon as they were old enough, as apprentices, often semi-slaves on a farm or in an urban workshop. It was improbable that they ever again saw their parents or even knew their identity.

Public opinion, backed by the State, thus began to exert influence on a person's private life and means of livelihood. It was wise to remain in one's own neighbourhood and to conform to the *mores* of the locality. The State was using the family to strengthen itself, and the State decided what was an acceptable style of family life. Generally, the State developed a more liberal attitude to marriage than in the rigid and unchanging code of the Catholic church, and the result was the growth of a morally permissive society in the classes unrestricted by extreme poverty and in a period of a changing and expanding economy. Elizabethan and Stuart literature and drama are full of illicit sex, perversions, and marital infidelity. The subjects are treated with humour or tolerance, but rarely with outraged condemnation. Alongside this strong vein of sexuality romantic love, culminating sometimes in marriage, and nearly always in consummation, came into its own. The traditional standards of benefits to the ancestral families as pre-eminent considerations in marriage arrangements were rejected, or at least presented as a quandary for lovers.

The Commonwealth imposed, or attempted to impose, strict morality by law enforcement. Carnal knowledge between unmarried persons was punishable by three months in prison, and in a characteristic policy of State interference in people's private lives, condonation of illicit sex by the parish constable —that is, his failure to arrest the culprits after he became aware of their offence—meant six months' imprisonment for him: twice the punishment of the actual offenders.

The zealots of the Cromwellian revolution may have practised within their own households what they preached outside, but the private lives of the mass of the people were largely unassailed. The rural population, when unaffected by State intereference as beggars or unemployed, enjoyed the best of both the old world and the new. The domination of the priest and the manorial lord had gone; the bigotry and moral strictness of the Puritans could be cautiously ignored. Consequently many new families were created mainly on the basis of mutual attraction between a man and a woman.

While the Puritans insisted that a wife must display the virtues of submission, obedience, and devotion to hard work, they were considerate of the status of a single woman. To some extent the spinster ceased to be a commodity for sale in the marriage market and enjoyed a few rights of her own. A single woman had for the first time protection against being forced to marry against her wishes or being inveigled into marriage almost before she knew it. A Marriage Act required proof of the consent of both parties, enforced a public announcement of an intended marriage, and permitted a Justice of the Peace to refuse to allow the wedding to take place if an interested person could show valid reason why it should not. A determined married woman, if she could get the support of the menfolk of her own family, might get a divorce, and re-marry later. If Milton had had his way divorce would have been authorised for mental cruelty as well as for sexual offences, but he was three centuries in advance of public opinion.

In contrast to a humane regard for a degree of liberty was the Puritans' religious zeal which approached fanaticism. It was inconvenient for them to advocate celibacy or revive the mediaeval theories about the innate evil of women because of the determination to break with every item of Roman Catholic dogma, but the words of the Bible were used to keep wives subservient.

This culture was exported and formed the basis of marriage and family patterns in the American colonies. The migrants were fleeing from unbearable conditions: poverty, social ostracism, religious intolerance. The goad driving them away from their birthplace was usually stronger than the magnet of a new life in an unknown country. For those who were married, emigration demanded mutual trust between husband and wife which transcended all traditional conventions about wifely subservience and masculine domination. For hundreds of young men and women colonisation was a form of elopement, offering the possibility of starting married life free from the well-nigh insuperable obstacles created by disapproving parents. William Penn searched England, Wales, Ireland, Holland, and Germany for men and women who wished to extricate themselves from social and family pressures and participate in his Holy Experiment. In no other way was it possible for the persecuted and underprivileged to find an adequate means of livelihood. In return for agreement to a period of indenture Penn's migrants were given a free passage across the Atlantic plus the promise of a gift of fifty acres of land when the indenture was completed. Within a year 4,000 people had settled in Pennsylvania, creating a culture in which class distinctions were small. Early marriage was encouraged as a partnership of two people rather than as an alliance between two families.

For mutual comfort and protection the settlers built their homes close to one another, creating villages, and during periods of severe weather, food shortage, or hostile activity by American Indians, the families tended to coalesce into one large unit. As everyone lived in much the same economic condition, and the chief distinction was in the strength and determination of the individual, the first marriages of the colonists and the founding of new families originated in mutual attraction. That affectionate overtures became an acceptable preliminary to marriage is indicated by the New England practice of bundling: the controlled intimacy in bed, with the couple partly dressed, for some hours of the night.

The wedding was regarded as a secular ceremony, and in the early years of colonisation, was conducted only by a civil magistrate. In a community where a rapid increase of population was vital, marriage was encouraged irrespective of the social and financial benefits which might accrue to the couple's families. Pennsylvanian bachelors were, in the eighteenth century, subjected to double taxes. For a woman to remain unmarried was anti-social in a community where men invariably outnumbered women. This hostility to unmarried women encouraged the persecution complex typified by charges of witchcraft and female immorality, both bringing vicious penalties. But married women enjoyed a degree of individual freedom they would never have known in Britain or Europe of that period. They were true partners in the family enterprises: running all the varied activities of an establishment which had to be self-sufficient in almost everything needed to maintain life.

This new and freely adopted type of family life, eminently suited for pioneer existence in a predominantly agricultural economy, had its rivals—attempts to turn back the clock and inaugurate the feudal system in the New World. In this clash of theories on social, economic, and family life were some origins of the American Civil War and the present barriers of outlook between North and South; the feudalistic concept, admittedly materialistically advantageous for the type of agriculture which climate and terrain favoured, naturally developed into a system of powerful and wealthy landowners whose existence depended on serfs—black and enslaved when white bondsmen and tied tenants were unavailable.

Maryland was a notable example of this New World feudalistic experiment and was originally planned as a manorial estate. It was the idea of Lord Baltimore to provide a refuge for persecuted Catholics, who were more agreeable to living under the old-fashioned feudalistic system of pre-Reformation times than the Dissenters and other independent Protestant groups who chose New England. Baltimore's scheme was to create a completely new class system, based mainly on the size of the settler's family and the number of employees he brought with him. Thus anyone bringing five workers could become the lord of a manor of a thousand acres, paying a token quit rent to Baltimore of £1 a year. Married status added a further hundred acres, and each child was valued at fifty acres. Maryland began with some sixty estates run on the feudal system. The manorial class were Catholic, but most of their vassals and tenants Protestant. Although there were objections by the priests on the one hand and the Puritans who moved into the colony on the other, religious tolerance was meticulously observed. Both sides were ready enough to regard land as the main consideration in matters of inheritance and marriage. Not only could the propertied classes increase their assets by arranging unions with the sons and daughters of neighbouring manors, but the birth of children meant further grants of territory from virtually illimitable acres of virgin land. Consequently, while marriage was regarded as a serious business to be carefully considered from the point of view of each family's future welfare, the social background of each partner was not of primary importance. Daughters did not need large dowries; younger sons without expectations were still potential landowners. Maryland deservedly became known as 'the best poor man's country in the world'.

Whatever direction the emigrant societies of the New World chose for their social culture the overall influence was democratic. The people chose their customs and taboos for themselves. Those who disapproved could move away. No irresistible pressures of poverty or tradition curbed individual desires and ambitions.

While this social revolution was slower in development in the Old World, eventual changes were inevitable. During the eighteenth century the decline of absolute monarchy became obvious in all well governed countries. Groups of men, representing families and a class rather than persons, shouldered more responsibilities of government. The medieval social and political structure in which privileged aristocrats and the clergy dominated national policy through a semi-divine monarch and a Pope who supported him were succumbing to the pressures of wealth created by a capitalist industrial and mercantile economy and larger populations. The Church's temporal power was no longer of great importance in the vigorous states of Europe. The aristocrat-capitalists depending on inheritance and investments were in a minority. A middle class was expanding in numbers and wealth, purchasing property from profits made by their services to the community. The majority of the population was still without any resources but growing in importance as the actual producers of wealth when the industrial revolution developed momentum. The other two classes sought both to control and exploit the lives of this mass of people. For the former purposes there were too many; for the latter too few. The State had to ensure that the masses did not destroy the culture created by the minority.

In England, far ahead in the industrial race, and experiencing the depressions and booms of an intricate trading economy, the eighteenth century saw the passage of a series of Acts, passed in 1722, 1782, and 1796, which widened the influence of legislation designed to help (and control) underprivileged families. The first of these Acts enabled Authority to invade the home and break up the family. Previously a man or woman needing help would usually be allowed to continue to live in his home, being given some kind of day work, or the materials for home industry, by the local overseer of the poor. Parliament then encouraged parishes to build workhouses and enacted that a man refusing to go and live there had no claim for relief, this effectively depriving him of his family life if the applicant was married.

The system was both harsh and expensive, with the additional defect that it did not solve the indigent family's problems. Some relaxation came with an Act in 1782 which allowed, but did not enforce, parishes to restrict residence in a workhouse to children, the incapacitated, and the aged. A fit man could continue to live at home while receiving relief or working at an allotted job. The latter was usually farm work, with the parish paying part of the man's wages and the farmer to whom he was hired the balance.

This system worked moderately well from the State's point of view until inflation during the Napoleonic Wars created an economic crisis in which a married agricultural labourer, with children, could not earn enough to feed his family, even in full-time work. The Government's solution was to draw up a table of wage rates based on the size of the worker's family and the price of bread. The difference between the wage actually paid by the farmer and the officially approved figure was a burden on the rates. This idea resulted in the degradation of decent families whose only sin was to have no savings or resources with which to meet the exorbitant cost of living. A family had to be in penury before there could be any official aid, but until the breadwinner was 'on the rates' he had little chance of finding employment. Farmers wanted labourers to whom they need pay as little as a third of the wages needed to maintain a family, the public paying the balance.

The miserable existence of the rural working classes and the waste of public money brought about a reactionary attitude, and in 1834 the Government set up the Poor Law Commission, answerable to nobody, to control the relief of the poor. It forbade relief to the needy in their own homes, and made life so unbearable that an appeal for public assistance was the last resort of a man with any self-respect and a vestige of hope. The solutions were to emigrate, move to the industrial towns, or take to crime. The overall result was the near-destruction of the rural family as it had existed since feudal times. For thirteen sorry years this Commission exerted its baleful influence, until in 1847 it was replaced by the Poor Law Board, a government department under control of Parliament and, of course, suject to criticism and change.

By this time theories born of the French revolution were also assailing the old concept that a marriage had to be an economic or social union of families. Rousseau had started the change with his insistence that 'the disintegration of the age-old basis of the family should in no wise create alarm'. One of the early actions of the Assembly in Paris was to abolish feudal rights and the laws of primogeniture, enforcing instead partition of most of a man's property among all his children. If the Declaration of the Rights of Man and the Citizen, 2 August 1789, did little to enhance the status of women with regard to their privileges in a man's world, the recognition of human freedom applied to every French citizen, male or female. Its virtue was that essentially it was a negative document enumerating what the State must not do instead of what the State could do. Regrettably some of the original declarations on personal liberty have since been subordinated in France to what is allegedly the interests of society as a whole, the invariable excuse for regimentation of individual life in a modern nation.

The 1789 Declaration inevitably aroused violent controversy in England. There were determined admirers bent on acclaiming it as an example for England to follow, and traditionalists who saw it as an evil to be rejected without discussion. The purpose seemed to be, at the level of family life, to transform the old-style paternalistic family into a miniature republic, with parental authority curbed and the indissolubility of marriage abolished. Children were to become equals as soon as they reached adult age. The family unit would have a defined life span, inaugurated by the marriage of two people, expanding with the birth of offspring, decreasing as the children became adults, and ending with the death of the surviving parent. In practice, of course, affection for kinsfolk and the desire to enjoy wealth and prestige ensured that the old style family culture survived, but it did so through the voluntary actions of the younger members, not at the command of the older ones.

The State thereupon assumed the right to break the unity of family members if the Establishment's opinion was that children would be better off when separated from their parents. Under George II in 1739 a statute provided that children of men or women convicted of criminal offences should be removed from parental care and apprenticed to an honest trade. This was the first time in England that the State sought to destroy a family for moral, as distinct from economic and health, reasons. As 'criminal offences' at the time ranged from minor pilfering to protests at work, and apprenticeship of young children was a euphemism for semi-slavery, the benefits to anyone but the Establishment were dubious. A year after this legislation the Courts were empowered to decide that a child, whether it owned property or not, could be removed from the control of a parent or guardian 'grossly unfit' or convicted of crime, and placed with a guardian nominated by the Court. Alongside this legislation there was the series of Factory Acts to curb the exploitation of children in industry. Necessary as such legislation was, the result was to curtail still further the traditional rights of parents over their children's lives. For decades the laws were modified during Parliamentary debate so that industry's prosperity was not too severely affected—the underlying factor transcending the ostensible purpose of child welfare.

The growth of industry had drawn thousands into the new towns—people whose English, Scottish and Irish forebears has lived in the same locality for generations. They settled in characterless dwellings with neighbours who were mostly strangers. The majority of these urban immigrants were illiterate and all were poor; communication either by letter or travel to visit their birthplace was difficult. Pride in family background weakened and died. The average workman and his wife lived a harsh and dreary existence among a crowd of other lonely people. All too frequently children came to be regarded as burdens and as soon as possible were turned into wage earners to contribute to the family's maintenance.

Yet the human spirit managed to surmount the appalling conditions of existence and the neuroses created when almost every quality of personal living was eroded. The urban workers had no home in the sense of the fabric lived in for generations by their forebears, and the bricks and mortar or lath and plaster of their tenements became known as a house, and the pathetically few possessions inside it were called the home by the wife—a custom which survives.

This was a justified attitude, for married women of the first half of the nineteenth century were gaining a measure of personal freedom and economic power. Both benefits were relative: neither they nor their husbands experienced much of either. But a wife had opportunities for employment outside the home just as her husband had. For hours every day she was an individual—exploited, overworked, ill-paid, but still a person in her own right.

The maintenance of the family was her responsibility. She balanced, or attempted to balance, the household budget. She chose the diet, contrived to clothe her man, her children, and herself; sometimes managed to save, and did miracles in creating an identity for her family. She was the social representative of the family: how the children looked and behaved; her husband's routine at work and at rest; the conditions and appearance of her home. All these were her responsibility. Out of a rootless, impoverished society the early Victorian working wife founded a steady, reliable, and usually conformist class. Her reward was long coming—but, perhaps without knowing it, she was paving the way for the women's movements for economic, legal, and political rights which began as the century drew to its close.

While small, rootless families were typical of social patterns in the new industrial towns of Northern and Midland England, in smaller towns where skilled crafts and trading on traditional lines were the chief sources of employment, family links from generation to generation survived and were often strengthened.

The serious-minded, God-fearing, resourceful and conscientious members of the new urban middle classes and skilled working classes observed a paternalistic culture in which the head of a family was also head of a firm—a sort of high priest of both. He presided over family prayers and business conferences with equal facility, in the assurance of his special position. They were 'in trade' and despised by the leisured upper class, but envied for their security and increasing influence.

The family firms created a grouping which extended beyond the kinsfolk of the owners. The paternalistic influence over employees was stern and unimaginative, but encouraged mutual loyalty. Workers were not summarily dismissed for inefficiency or mistakes, but penalised in much the same way as junior family members or the household servants of the owner of the firm. An employee's children had a much better chance of getting a job in the same firm than a stranger, and the firms themselves were proudly under the direction of one family and remained so for generation after generation. To change the family name by adding 'and Son' was the ambition of every business head. Finance needed for expansion was provided by relatives or close friends, who became actively interested shareholders, while those unable to work were aided by a present of shares to provide them with an income. The whole enterprise was a form of extended tribal family, with the typical suspicion of strangers and the traditional sense of unity among the members.

Towards the middle of the nineteenth century limited liability companies, with shareholders who had little interest in the welfare of the employees or in the company's business methods so long as profits were good, began to replace these old-fashioned family firms. Corporations, cartels, combines, and monopolies put a dynamic force into the creation of wealth. Labour and management drew apart, each side becoming strangers to the other, and more and more frequently regarding one another as enemies.

The mass of workers, now urban dwellers, sought a corporate identity in unions, where the feeling of belonging to a social unit as well as a militant organisation was typified by one member calling another 'brother', still preferred to the communist-style 'comrade'. A further trend towards creating group alliances of working class people was seen in the phenomenal growth of fraternal orders and friendly societies. Some of the fraternal orders were a type of semi-secret society with objects which were largely social and convivial. The more popular friendly societies brought working people together for mutual protection against the miseries of accident, sickness and old age—precisely the tragic eventualities of life which had been dealt with by tribal groups and large families since prehistoric times.

The social and economic changes in nineteenth-century Britain meant that a feeling of insecurity was ever-present in men's minds. It was fought off by stern discipline, enthusiasm for the hell fire type of religion, and determination to build up a strong social unit originating in the home and through whatever class-conscious organisation would best serve men's interests. The basis of this planned stability was the Victorian family, a patriarch type of social unit of a kind hardly known since the Roman Empire declined. It was founded on materialistic considerations masquerading as virtues. As always, when such a culture is dominant, sexual appetites had to be regarded as inimical to the carefully planned family structure. The Victorian men's attitude to women was that they were in reality as well as in law among the chattels of a father or husband. Yet at the same time women's better education and the repercussions of the French revolutionaries and their intellectual allies ensured that they could not be treated like animals. The facile solution was to place women in two differing groups.

One, which included every man's daughter, was to idealise femininity as almost sexless. A woman's innocence and virtues were so strongly protected that she had to be courted with a mealy-mouthed travesty of what was believed to be the gallantry of the Middle Ages. She was asked for her hand in marriage, but no one mentioned her body—its importance she learned on her wedding night when she might suffer legalised rape. Somehow, thanks to the eternal resourcefulness of woman, she emerged unscathed to bear a regiment of children and to rear them efficiently and lovingly. Moreover, she became the ambassador of the family. The Victorian wife was the person who created social status.

The second group were not regarded as suitable for marriage in the meaning of the word to the Victorians. They were, as one prosperous merchant put it, 'for use'. Alongside the prudery which was the mark of responsible society from the palace down to the back-to-back houses of the industrial towns, there flourished a prurience which supported commercialised sex and pornography on a scale hardly known in Britain before or since. In 1857 the medical journal, the *Lancet*, estimated that one house in sixty in London was a brothel, and the city provided a living for 80,000 prostitutes, equal to one in sixteen of the female inhabitants of all ages. The Chief of Police in New York City estimated in 1856 that the city had 5,000 prostitutes, 378 Houses of Prostitution and 100 Houses of Assignation.[2] (A police report at the end of the nineteenth century estimated the total of New York City prostitutes at 40,000.) In the industrial towns seduction of young girls in the factories and mills was routine practice, usually regarded by the victims as a necessary payment to ensure security of employment and to obtain favours from the overseers. When records were started in 1870 the nation expressed horror (though no surprise) that 6 per cent of all births in the United Kingdom were illegitimate, a proportion not exceeded until the end of World War II, and then only temporarily.

The Establishment remained largely indifferent to the moral and economic plight of women who were unable to marry. But their champions had been emerging for decades; they were persistent and patient. The panaceas they later offered for social evils were varied: emancipation for all women, married or single, rich or poor; destruction of the family as it was then known; political revolution. Only the middle classes held fast to their ideals of the nuclear family and rejected most of the suggested innovations. It was a social unit stronger perhaps than even the Victorian paterfamilias realised.

A further revolutionary change during the nineteenth century was the attempt to control the size of the family. Abortion and infanticide, as we have seen, were the crude but effective methods of restricting the number of offspring up to the Christian era. In addition, the Egyptians, Greeks and Romans had sufficient knowledge of the mechanics of conception to devise methods of preventing it, but these were generally unknown in early and medieval Christendom, and where Roman methods were read in manuscript the monkish students regarded them as taboo, not only as a means of destroying the seeds of human life, but as encouraging sexual intercourse merely for pleasure. A welter of folklore, handed down from mother to daughter, provided dubious methods of birth control. The ideas were, of course, largely ineffective, as women of today who still heed them discover. But the 'safe period' of low fertility was ascertainable by experience, and this was respected by those men who displayed exceptional consideration for their wives, and more widely by illicit lovers fearful of discovery and punishment.

In England the idea that births should be limited as a policy of State had become a topic of controversy in 1801, when Thomas Malthus, a clergyman and political economist, published his 'Essay on the Principle of Population as it Affects the Future Improvement of Society'.[3] His cure for overpopulation was moral restraint, which meant late marriage, sexual abstinence during marriage, and, of course, chastity by single persons. As is the widespread view today, restriction of the number of offspring was, in Malthus's opinion, the duty of the poor, whose fecundity was the reason for their poverty. His proposals could have worked only by interference by the State in changing the minimum age for marriage and imposing heavier penalties for fornication and adultery, with the Churches restoring and enforcing the medieval taboos against the amount of intercourse after marriage. Neither State nor

G

Church could at that time of change and unrest have believed it advisable or effective to make any new laws.

It has been calculated that up to the sixteenth century the population increase in England was achieved by an average of 2.6 offspring per family, and to produce this number of children surviving to adulthood a woman bore six children. No restrictions on sexual activity within or outside marriage could have materially changed the 2.6 figure of long-surviving maternities for the average woman, and the steady, if slow, improvement in the expectation of life was resulting in more children surviving until puberty at the time of the Malthus campaign.

Family limitation, which could not be enforced from outside the family, therefore began from within—by the quiet determination of the wives. The reformer Francis Place launched the so-called neo-Malthusian movement with a pamphlet published in 1823 in which he gave the woman's case for contraception, a scientifically sound argument which was dismissed by the medical world of his day. His 'diabolical handbills' were circulated in the industrial towns, passed from wife to wife, and read by those who were literate to those who were not.

If Place experienced little but hostility in England his ideas were studied sympathetically and seriously in America. Back to England came the first real manual on birth control, innocuously titled *The Fruits of Philosophy*, with a more instructive sub-heading *Or the Private Companion of Young Married People*. Its author was a Boston physician, Dr Charles Knowlton. For year after year some 700 copies of the pamphlet were sold in Britain, the purchasers for the most part being social workers and political reformers who distributed them to others to read to their women friends. Then, in 1875, Charles Bradlaugh and Annie Besant were prosecuted on the grounds of obscenity for circulating Knowlton's work. The Establishment's real objection was that the circulation was among the working classes. The publicity about the book sent sales soaring to best-seller dimensions, more than 125,000 being sold in the weeks between the announcement of the charges and the trial. Both defendants were found guilty and sentenced to a heavy fine and imprisonment, but the convictions were quashed on technical grounds.[4]

Although without exception the Churches condemned artificial methods of birth control, the existence of means of limiting the size of the family was now an irrefutable and ascertainable fact. In 1870-2, before the Besant-Bradlaugh trial, the live births per thousand women in the United Kingdom had been 151.5, ten years later it had dropped to 145.7 and in 1890-2 to 129.2; in the United States in 1890 there were 139 live births per thousand white women. Married women were at long last gaining a personal power they had never known in the history of family life: the knowledge of how to control their fecundity. The growing sense of mutual respect among many married people ensured that for the first time couples were planning, or at least attempting to plan, the size of their families.

The governments of countries in an advanced state of civilisation, expanding industrially and by conquest of less progressive peoples, wanted manpower for the factories and what later became regarded as cannon fodder. The Churches, battling to retain their hold on the personal behaviour of their restless adherents, tried to maintain the spiritual and moral *status quo*. Families had to be large, no matter what the price the individual members had to pay, if the old order was to survive. It was the commencement, or perhaps resumption, of a long battle between the individual and those who desired to control his existence.

Notes and Bibliography for this chapter are on pp174-5.

6 *Men and Women in Social Revolt*

The ideals about equality and the rights of the individual which were so energetically voiced in late Victorian times, in all Western countries, did not extend to demotion of the male as the dominant sex, with the husband the master in his home as well as in the workaday world. Most of the pioneer Socialists were adamant that a woman's place was in the home, and the fact that she often had to go out and earn wages in order that a family could survive was proof of the faults of a society which they wanted to change. Sex equality was so revolutionary an idea that it was usually dismissed as the absurd notion of a few bright young ladies of the aristocracy and rebellious wives of middle class professional men.

In England legislation of benefit to the married woman was largely concerned with property—action inspired by the middle and upper classes anxious to guard the inviolability of the family line on the female side. Thus an Act passed in 1857 provided that a deserted wife could apply for a protection order to ensure that property she acquired after her desertion belonged to her as completely as if she were single. Two years later this right was extended to a wife whose husband had been convicted of a serious assault on his wife. She could apply to the courts for exemption from the need to cohabit with her husband and, as regards property thereafter obtained, could be regarded as unmarried.

The Married Women's Property Act of 1870 conferred a degree of economic independence on all married women. A wife could retain all her savings in bank deposits and her earnings; the rents and profits of all landed property she owned (but her husband could administer the estate); and all personal property coming to her after marriage not in excess of £200. By a subsequent Act of 1882 a married woman was given absolute ownership of all property belonging to her before marriage or obtained afterwards. A husband no longer had legal rights over her property. Thus for the first time in history a British wife became a person in law. With the privileges came responsibilities. If she had property she had to maintain a pauper husband and support her children and grandchildren.

All this was of little import to the mass of working-class men and women. Working wives rarely had any personal property, and they had always been obliged to use their wages to help support their families. Many were accustomed to being the sole wage earner in periods of economic depression, when women retained low-paid jobs while men were unemployed. The protection of the working-class family would have been more effective if the deleterious effects of exhausting work for women had been tackled. The worst results had of course been dealt with by banning women from mine work (they still continued to work underground dressed as men or boys). Characteristic of a tender regard for the employers' interests was the Act of 1891 which prohibited employers 'knowingly' permitting a female to work in factory or workshop within four weeks of giving birth to a child. Efforts to extend the ban to a week or two before birth were rejected.

Working women had to create their own champions and fight for the right to vote on equal terms with men in union affairs as vigorously as for a Parliamentary vote. Two women,

Eva Gore-Booth and Esther Roper, self-appointed champions of the women workers of Lancashire's cotton mills, gave a first hint of the political potential of the women's vote. They persuaded women trade unionists to give a vote of approval for adopting David Shackleton as candidate for Clitheroe in a 1902 by-election. Shackleton had pledged himself to press for women's suffrage (though in fact he subsequently did little about it). The women's vote proved decisive in giving Shackleton the chance to campaign for the seat. Four years later, in the 1906 general election, the working women of Wigan found a man, Thorley Smith, prepared to stand as 'Women's Candidate and Independent Labour', the independence an enforced status because his support of the feminists meant he was rejected by the local miners' union and trades council. He failed to win this traditionally Tory seat but beat the Liberal candidate in an historic election which swept the Liberal party to power. Smith's 2,205 votes were in effect the token votes of the 96,000 women trade unionists of Lancashire who had managed to persuade their menfolk to vote for a women's candidate. The result was regarded by all political parties as little short of sensational and an ominous pointer to the future. Their reaction was to intensify resistance to women's emancipation. The domestic rows which followed this intrusion of women into trade union affairs and politics may be visualised, but the women were the victors. They were exploiting their economic independence as wage earners and joint supporters of the family, and were criticised for it as being unwomanly and damaging to the traditional ways of family life.

For the women of the middle and upper classes better education was an effective means of enjoying independence if they did not marry, and a degree of equality if they did. Queen's College, Bedford College, and Cheltenham Ladies' College had been founded in the middle of the century for the fortunate few girls with fathers enlightened and wealthy enough to enrol them. Girton College for women opened Cambridge to women in 1872 and was quickly followed by

Newnham. London University allowed women to sit for degrees in 1878, followed by Lady Margaret Hall and Somerville Hall at Oxford. Education was producing an elite class of women who furthered the advance of feminism and the corresponding decline in the male-dominated family.

Everywhere old standards were crumbling. New writers—Wilde, Wells and Shaw—were assailing the inviolable status of the family with wit, cynicism or objective criticism. Greatly respected women like Florence Nightingale were openly questioning the accepted idealistic picture of the home. 'I know nothing like the petty grinding tyranny of a good English family,' she wrote. 'The vacuity and boredom of this [family] existence are sugared over by false sentiment.'

The emphasis on political emancipation by what came to be known as the Suffragette movement was partly an attack on the existing code of family life.[1] It seemed to the feminists that political power was the only way to give a wife and daughter some of the freedom that a husband and a son enjoyed. The opponents were without exception those who wished that the patriarchal society should continue, whatever political party was in power.

Victoria, queen and empress of nearly one-third of the world, without a husband for thirty years of her career, and despotic in her control of her children and her Ministers, nevertheless let it be known that in her opinion the campaign for female emancipation was a 'mad wicked folly of Woman's Rights with all its attendant horrors, on which her poor feeble sex is bent, forgetting every sense of womanly feeling and propriety. God created men and women different: then let them remain in their own position'.[2]

The reference to God's design for the inferiority (and wickedness) of women was, of course, a cogent if facile argument in an age when most people still piously accepted the literal truth of every word of the Bible. Such men who were liberal enough to admit that the women had a case did their best to contrive a compromise between bigotry and justice.

The inferiority of Eve, through being constructed from Adam's rib, was explained away by the theory that the Hebraic word for 'rib' had been mistranslated; it actually meant 'half', and woman was therefore precisely a moiety of the original man-woman whole. A few bold spirits described that much-quoted difference of the divine creation as concerning only the mammary glands and the sexual organs. Scientifically, they insisted, it was as ridiculous to suggest that a woman's intelligence, imagination, or emotional needs were different from a man's as to talk about a female lung or a female liver having a different function from those organs in the male body. There was, in fact, no scientific justification for a Victorian woman who got married to be condemned, as John Stuart Mill put it, 'as the personal body servant of a despot'.[3]

Feminists were emerging as enemies of the very existence of marriage, and were calling the family home not a haven, but a dungeon. Some of the 'new women' were suggesting that a woman should be the one to decide when conception might take place, and a few advocated that the decision could be made whether the woman was married or single. The view, usually unspoken, that a woman was a sexually activated person just as much as a man spelt the doom of the conventional picture of the perfect woman being pure, innocent and sexless, yet loving and feminine. Once sex became mentionable, men who were really misogynists but purported to be defenders of a stable society could use it to condemn women more harshly than ever, and this masculine attitude persisted long after more equality for women in social and economic matters had been accepted as just.

Whatever views an unbiased person held on the feminine rights controversy, it was impossible to ignore the fact that the assault on the established structure of family life was being encouraged by revolutionary theories which forecast the doom of a capitalist society. The ideas of Karl Marx and Friedrich Engels, and the host of political philosophers who followed them, could be criticised as more destructive than constructive. As society had to be changed, everything which society practised and approved had to go. Any human association, thriving with little interference by the State or alternatively protected by a political system which was corrupt, was automatically suspect to the Marxian mind. As the family was an autonomous group it was therefore a menace. Whether its object was the protection of property, the maintenance of social prestige, or just a miniature society of freely associating individuals, it was regarded as inimical to the supremacy of the proletariat.

The revolutionists' assault on the family brought firm reaction from the established culture. It was compelled to increase its ostensibly benign interference in family affairs in order to safeguard the traditional pattern. The past indicated that throughout human history the communal body—clan, tribe, or nation—had concerned itself closely with marriage, but once the marriage had taken place, the newly formed family was left to its own devices, except for the fact that its fragmentation was made difficult. Only in weak or dying communities was the break-up of marital partners and the transfer of children to the care of others outside the family tolerated without hindrance. Experience had shown that stable families, whatever the position of individuals in it, were the bricks of a stable society. One could not survive without the other.

The growth of mass populations of largely propertyless persons, no longer disciplined by serfdom or blinded by ignorance, and almost entirely dependent on earning money with which to purchase the necessities of life, forced the State to consider the private lives of these people. They could not succeed in the struggle for existence unaided, and their usually miserable lives made them useful tools in the hands of malcontents and agitators.

The late Victorian method of strengthening the family cult was genuinely inspired by humane considerations, but strongly influenced by a belief in the virtues of discipline and

the benefits of the class system. Voluntary aid on behalf of
families too poor or too irresponsible adequately to care for
their children pursued a policy of filling the stomach and
dragooning the spirit. Perhaps unwillingly, many of the
charitable organisations endeavoured to create a corporate
spirit among the young which rivalled or even eradicated
family loyalties. The Girls' Friendly Society, founded in 1875,
was at first restricted to girls in factories and domestic service,
and it endeavoured to help these exploited young women to
have a better life, provided they meekly resigned themselves
to occupations which by their nature continued to exploit
them. The Boys' Brigade, originating in Glasgow in 1883,
operated on a mixture of military discipline and religious piety
which again inculcated acceptance of a social order with a
mixture of Christian resignation to the inevitable and a bold
spirit in the face of adversity. More practical, though aid was
dependent on a gesture of religious acquiescence and a readi-
ness to identify with the movement, were the penny meals for
children and the needy organised by the Salvation Army. The
Boy Scouts, started in 1907, and the Girl Guides three years
later, were midde-class organisations which, significantly,
strengthened the members' loyalty to family life rather than
providing a contrast to it, as was the case of organisations pur-
porting to aid the deprived.

In the latter half of the nineteenth century any intelligent
observer could see that a generation of millions was growing
up in industrial savagery. Illiteracy was the normal state of
the children in the industrial towns and most rural areas. In
Glasgow, where as late as 1861 an estimated hundred thous-
and people were living in one-room houses, often fifteen to a
room and consisting of several adults and offspring whose
paternity was unknown, there were children who had no given
names or surnames but answered to nicknames like dogs.

Schools charging from $\frac{1}{2}$p to 2p per week started after
1870. Even the lowest fee was beyond the resources of a father
with three or four children and earning only 75p per week.

When school attendance became compulsory in England and Wales after 1880 impoverished parents were as much bewildered as resentful at this official interference in their children's lives. Truancy was widespread, and could mean the despatch of the erring child to an industrial school, the forerunner of the approved school. Parents, if they were poor, were no longer sole arbiters of their children's activities even if they committed no crime, were well fed and clothed, and healthy.

Official welfare, such as compulsory education, medical examinations of schoolchildren, control over the fostering of children, followed by the adoption of Germany's state pension scheme for the aged poor, and sick pay for workers, steadily enlarged the State's encroachment on the family. Desirable and humane as all these developments were, they did enforce change on the traditional ways of family life. The travesty of existence which the State's welfare legislation was intended to improve may have been more nearly eradicated from the national scene. But there was a cost in a deterioration of pride, duty, and self-respect. A divisive force was in the background of every home: the State was becoming the partner of every family head, and was steadily advancing to be the senior one. Controversy over the affairs of family members could have only one outcome: the family head lost the argument. The State knew best, and had the force of law to prove it.

Apart from the way offspring should be reared, the State was also dictating the attitude to be adopted towards their mother. Not until 1925 was a woman with a living husband granted rights on the custody and control of her children, though in 1886 a widow was given those rights. Previously the paternalistic domination of family life had given a husband the sole right to nominate the guardian of his children after his death, and he could exclude his wife without giving any reason.

Five years later an ordinary woman achieved a degree of sexual freedom for wives. 'Restitution of conjugal rights' had previously meant precisely what the phrase implied; a wife could be forced back to her husband's bed and board. A Mrs Jackson, aided by her own relatives, fought for her rights as an English subject, irrespective of her sex. She had been kidnapped by her estranged husband and his friends, confined in a house under restraint by a 'nurse', and told she would not be freed until she agreed to resume cohabitation with her husband. The case went to the Court of Appeal where Mrs Jackson was granted a writ of *habeas corpus* compelling her release.

~ The effects of the first world war on family life in the belligerent nations are too well known to need elaboration. Two factors were of major and lasting impact: the man's obligation to leave his home and join the national fighting forces, and the resultant necessity for his wife to take over all responsibilities of the family and, in many cases, to earn its means of support. The service allowances for wives and children were too scanty to do more than ward off starvation, and women moved into work which had hitherto been exclusively masculine. Single women, many from families who would in normal conditions have forbidden paid employment for their daughters away from parental control, enjoyed the wartime experience of being self-supporting and free to do much as they pleased.

The right to vote for women over thirty which was their reward in 1919 was a wives' charter, for the majority of the emancipated women were of course married, and fully aware from experience of the faults and omissions of the State in the protection and improvement of feminine rights. While the comparatively high age groups of the new voters meant that conservative opinions predominated, and security of family life was regarded as the vital interest of every wife and mother, the younger generation of women saw their imminent political emancipation as a gate to freedom from the thraldom of old-fashioned marriage and wifely subservience.

The 1920s brought ideas, startling enough to merit wide-

spread discussion in the press, for trial marriages and companionate marriages.[4] Most of them originated outside Britain.
A Professor Fetscher in Germany took a poll of the sexual
behaviour of betrothed couples and reported the obvious: in
all strata of German society many of these young people
anticipated marriage, often without parental disapproval. With
typical Teutonic anxiety to have everything regulated, he
advocated that an engagement should legally permit sexual
intercourse. In the USA the Episcopal Church attempted to
regularise illicit sexual unions, and a Dr M. M. Knight suggested a partnership formed solely for the comfort and
pleasure of a man and a woman and having nothing whatever
to do with the creation or maintenance of a family.[5] These
theories were inevitably condemned as immoral and decadent,
the attacks giving them far wider publicity than perhaps they
merited. Their important effect was to confirm the private
beliefs of millions of young people that sexual attraction was
becoming the key factor in marriage. This attitude, however
selfish, was remorselessly replacing all concepts of putting
family considerations first and emotional desires second.

By all those who believed that the post-war world had to
be changed to destroy the evils which had led to global war,
and that the relationships of men and women would have to
conform to some new—and State-directed—pattern, the policies in the young Soviet Union were studied with care.
Unfortunately for all the radical and anarchistic critics of marriage and family life, in the Marx-Engels tradition, the Russian
social experiments soon proved so changeable that at best they
offered a lesson on what to avoid rather than what to adopt.

Marriage in the Soviet Union is now based on a series of
laws passed in 1926. The minimum age is eighteen, though
local authorities are allowed to reduce the age to seventeen
for women, and in some of the eastern republics the traditional minimum age of sixteen for women has been retained.
Marriage between relatives in the direct line of descent and
between half-brother and half-sister is not allowed. Bigamy is

forbidden, but is not punishable unless it supports a survival of tribal custom, which the regime has always attempted to stamp out.

The traditional wedding in pre-revolutionary Russia was a religious ceremony, and no other form was recognised. The reverse now holds true, and the only legal union is one conducted and registered by the State. This was enforced by a law passed in 1944, altering the code of 1926, which recognised a *de facto* union as having the same legal status as a legally registered marriage. Children born to single women or widows are not treated as illegitimate. The official description is that they are fatherless.

The Russian family is now almost restored to a status it enjoys in capitalist countries. Decrees passed in 1943 and 1945 completely changed the original policy adopted in conformity with the Marxist theory that under communism the family would wither away. The wartime legislation approved possessions being handed down from one generation to another. A family head can now leave as much as he has without the State taking any of the inheritance apart from a registration fee up to 10 per cent of the value of the estate. This regard for personal property—and so for the continued existence of the family—was adopted under the New Economic Policy of 1921, and reversed the official action which immediately followed the Revolution, when laws specifically abolished inheritance.

The vigorous Russian peasant family unit is often part of a kinship group very little different in make-up from that existing for century after century in agricultural economies. The Kolkhoz is a cooperative farming community consisting of a village or a group of hamlets, and though every Kolkhoz is managed by Party officials the work force is made up largely of kinsmen, not least because membership is automatic for every child born in the village, and because of the difficulty of leaving the locality. These peasants represent at least a third of the population of the Soviet Union, so their three-generation families, with strong links through inter-marriage with all others in the community, are maintaining what is really a very ancient form of family life. Neither starvation, purges, nor war have caused any fundamental change in this social institution.

The inhabitants of rural Russia, whatever description they are given and however efficiently indoctrinated, remain devotees of marriage to strengthen family ties and of families enduring much in order that communal kinship may survive. For these millions all the ideological 'freedoms' from marital bonds and family laws are mainly of theoretical interest. For the urban population and the myriads of State employees, however, communism has brought major changes in their personal and social lives.

Among the experiments of the founders of the Soviet Union were the advocacy of free love and the virtual abolition of permanent marriage by making divorce a minor formality. The champion of free love was Aleksandra Kollontay, a revolutionary who was active in Europe and the USA before the first world war. Her bizarre theories on marriage and sex enjoyed great popularity among feminists both in Russia and the West, and were respected because of her place in the Soviet hierarchy, despite the eventual disapproval of Lenin. Ostensibly her aim was to free women from the thraldom of marriage and to weaken family ties as inimical to Marxism. Her 'Winged Eros' idea was that everyone should be free to associate with other members of the opposite sex for as short or as long a period as mutually desired, and with several persons simultaneously for different reasons: intellectual, political, social, and sexual. Human nature being what it is, the popular enthusiasm was for the sexual reasons, and ephemeral liaisons created vast problems regarding the welfare of the 'fatherless' children born as a result.

After the 1917 Revolution divorce was allowed for one or both parties without the need to give a reason. Nine years later it was not even necessary to register a divorce. Stalin reduced the chaos by making registration obligatory in 1936, with both parties to the case present in court. In 1944 the original policy was reversed, and for a time divorce became almost as difficult as in the average Catholic dominated country. It was available only to those of wealth or political influence.[6] The People's Courts, in practice the only ones available for ordinary citizens, cannot grant a divorce; they must try to effect a reconciliation. Those who are able to proceed to a higher court can expect to get a divorce only if the family structure has been destroyed beyond all hope of repair, and even then no divorce will be granted if the reason for the family's break-up can be shown to be the fault of the person applying for the divorce. The generally accepted offences against a married partner—adultery, cruelty, perversion, and desertion—in capitalist countries carry no impact in the Soviet courts. The well-being and survival of the family has become more important than the happiness of the individual in it—an attitude which would have infuriated Karl Marx.

As a mother the Russian woman can gain prestige if she is prepared to produce large numbers of children. Unmarried mothers receive an allowance beginning with the first child; married mothers for the fourth and subsequent children. An elaborate system of awards and honours culminates in the title of Mother Heroine for the woman who has ten children. Despite this sort of encouragement the birth increase per thousand of population has dropped from forty-seven prior to the Revolution to about twenty-six since the war.

Contraceptives are available, but their use is not encouraged. Abortion is legal and was originally free. In the early 1930s abortions were more numerous than births in Moscow and some other large towns, and as a result it was made illegal in 1936. Twenty years later it was again legalised, but was no longer free.

As soon as a child is old enough to be educated the State steps in. The official attitude is that the rearing of children is a duty to be shared equally by parents and society, with society (ie the State) readily exerting greater influence as the child gets older. Between the ages of six and nine the child is expected to join the October Children organisation; from nine to fourteen he is in the Young Pioneers; from fourteen he is in the Komsomol. These organisations provide a nation-wide influence with a uniform ideology, and members are taught that if the influence of the family deviates from the official line they should obey the organisation and not the family. One of the heroes of Russian children is Pavlik Moro-zov, a Young Pioneer murdered by relatives after he had betrayed his parents to the police for their anti-Soviet activi-ties. Morozov has statues in his memory and many of the Young Pioneer groups are named after him.

The USSR, as one of the two super-powers in the modern world, exerting its ideological influences on at least a third of the world's peoples, has experimented with profound changes in mankind's family and marriage customs, and may continue to do so. That ideas which at the time appeared beneficial to the individual and advantageous to the State have been largely abandoned, and traditional customs have been revived and subsequently given the cachet of legal approval, is a pointer to the probably ephemeral nature of the more extreme experi-ments in the capitalist West.

As at all stages of civilisation, religious beliefs and laws have moulded the family cultures of the ancient nations of the Orient. These customs may indeed have a world-wide influ-ence in the future as the West abandons many of its social traditions, whereas the Eastern nations, while westernising themselves economically and technically, apparently intend to maintain their traditions so far as marriage and family are concerned.

Notes and Bibliography for this chapter are on pp175-6.

H

7 *Oriental Concept of Sex and Family Life*

The growth of nationalism, and an already increasing disillusion as regards the Western way of life, could well mean a reactionary trend in Arab and Asiatic countries. By the same token the widespread desire of younger people in the materialistic West for mystical experience, through experiments with drugs, foolishly with bizarre occult pseudo-sciences such as astrology, is indicative of a growing preoccupation with the more satisfying and worth-while cults of the East, which seem bound to have increasing influence on the white races.

Ancient customs have survived more tenaciously in most countries of the Orient than in the West, partly because the patterns of civilisation were established earlier than in most of Europe or the New World, and their religious beliefs have continued to exert a strong influence over the social and political activities of their adherents, except where communist regimes have been instituted and have endeavoured to suppress priestly influence. Some religions have endured almost unchanged for a very long period. Buddhism was founded in the sixth century BC, Confucianism in the same period. The literature of classical Hinduism originated as early as 1500 BC. Only Islam is comparatively new, but the Old Testament provided the background for Mohammed's teaching, with Abraham the father of the Arab peoples as he was of the Jews.

Understandably the customs of Oriental family life vary greatly from nation to nation, and within each nation, even if the major religions are international. Due to the influence of the West, at first by conquest, colonisation and missionary work, and more recently by trade and political alliance, the white man's type of family structure has sometimes been voluntarily adopted as the ideal and almost as often forced on the population through the imposition of Western-type laws and by Western-type industrialisation. The main change has been from a family pattern which was originally one of polygamy to monogamy. Even where the religion permits more than one wife or the social culture regards concubinage as acceptable, the monogamous family is now overwhelmingly in the majority.

This change may be morally desirable, if only because monogamy enhances the status of women, but it can weaken traditional ways of living and create problems which the West has known for centuries and failed completely to solve. In practice polygamy has been an economic benefit to peoples lacking machinery and living in an underpopulated and harsh environment. Cultivation of land and animal husbandry were improved if there was a source of plentiful woman-power. A man with several wives, and proportionately more children, had a source of increased wealth and therefore of prestige and power. Only in Oriental countries where wealth was amassed over generations did the women of a polygamous family become sexual toys in the popular Western concept of the harem. It is an arguable point whether monogamy and machinery are marks of a finer civilisation than a culture where there is unremitting toil but awareness of a place for all women in a complicated polygamous family culture.

The original and basic pattern of family life has survived in non-Christian countries despite the decline in polygamy. The Asiatic family remains largely patriarchal and marriage is a family matter, often with a betrothal agreed, or actually conducted as a solemn formality, before the boy and girl concerned can have any feelings about it and certainly few rights to voice them.

A wife expects to live under some degree of segregation. If her husband is wealthy her place is the home; if he is poor, her place is in the field or workshop. There is in these attitudes some status for a wife, setting her above single women: she is both a possession protected and isolated so as not to arouse the lust and envy of other men, and she is a valuable economic asset. She gains, too, an importance and prestige as the mother of sons. Now that the strict segregation of wives has been relaxed except among the poorest of rural people and in a few religious sects, women of the Orient and the Near East have gained a degree of freedom as persons; it is doubtful whether they have gained much as wives.

Of all Asiatic nations the Japanese have been the most successful in maintaining the ancient stability of the family while adopting the cult of Western-style industrial civilisation. Wisely, the American victors declined to remove the father figure of Japan, the Emperor, merely requiring the modification of some of the trappings of divine royalty. The Japanese remain conscious members of a family of 90 millions. Within this body are distinguished families rigorously guarding their ancient prestige, and the newer families identified with commercial undertakings. Instead of anonymous boards of directors and unapproachable managements as so often exist in the West, the mammoth industrial and commercial complexes have a father figure, at one and the same time the arbitrary autocrat and personal guardian of every employee. Workers are perfectly content to be ordered to gather for what are really family prayers at the start of each shift, to wear company approved clothes, to eat company food and to be housed in company living quarters. Courtship is spontaneous but common sense and propinquity encourage the choice of a marriage partner within the company's work force. The company will arrange the wedding, allocate a home, in due time arrange a place for retirement, and, finally organising the funeral ceremony.

As in all Asiatic countries, religion has been the force fashioning the family structure in Japan. While there is today complete religious freedom in the country, Shintoism, with its subsequent mixture of Buddhism, consciously or unconsciously directs the behaviour of most Japanese throughout their lives. The mixture of worship of nature and ancestors encourages the paternalistic type of family. The regard for the head of the family for generation after generation is so great that in important families prestige for the children may be restricted to the eldest son only. The old nickname for all sons and daughters, other than the principal heir, was 'cold rice', implying that they are fed only after the father and eldest son have taken what they needed.

In such a male-dominated family the wife inevitably takes a lowly position. The legal equality of the sexes has not materially altered her submissive role. A major part of a girl's education is concerned with 'womanly duties', which are not concerned only with housewifery, cooking, motherhood and similar practical activities: the Japanese girl is taught that her role is to suppress much of her own individualism in order to benefit her husband and family.

Conditioning from birth enables the Japanese girl, however equal to her brother she may find herself in the opportunities of earning her living while she is single, to regard her subservient role in family life with equanimity once she is married. Her husband is usually one she personally wants to marry, though he may have been introduced through a professional matchmaker and she is unlikely even to think of marrying without the approval of both her own and her prospective husband's families. After marriage she is assured of respect from all her relatives. Her children will be well cared for and given great affection despite the preference for the eldest son in matters of education and privileges. Japan's severest critics admit that the country is a paradise for young children.

The underlying and usually unspoken regard for a Japanese wife and mother is encouraged by Shinto beliefs. The principal divinity is a goddess, Amaterasu, and there is among Japanese men a feeling amounting to veneration for the sexual pleasures a loving wife can confer. One of the many Shinto gods brought a divine prostitute with him when he descended to earth. Temple prostitutes exalted sexual intercourse into a ritual until the thirteenth century, and relics of religious sexual activities survive among the geishas.

Japan is notable as an Asiatic country which has practised monogamy for many centuries. Divorce by mutual consent was available long before any major country in the West even considered it, and though the trivial grounds on which a couple could legally separate were restricted after 1897, the availability of divorce protected wives from an unendurable situation or the degrading insult of having to accept concubines in the household.

A remarkable custom is the right of a Japanese woman to be the founder of a new family. A single woman may adopt children. She is then known as the house head of a legally recognised family. True to the paternalistic tradition, the eldest adopted son will, on reaching maturity, become head of the family, replacing the mother in this role.

While Japan has so far succeeded in combining industrial capitalism without abandoning or even seriously changing her social traditions her powerful neighbour, the Republic of China, has chosen a different policy to achieve much the same end. Evidence about the life of the individual in China may be suspect, but only unthinking anti-communists can wholly believe that one of the world's most ancient and convention-ridden nations has in the space of a few years thrown away every tradition to adopt the teachings of Karl Marx, or that a deeply devout nation has forgotten or rejected every tenet of its beliefs. Behind the machinery of propaganda, and within the pages of the famous red book, there is plenty of evidence to the contrary. The New China is the Old China seen in a mirror, and the distortions do not alter the reality of the persistence of the object in the image.

According to Chinese legend Hu-hsi, the first Chinese emperor of whom details survive, who lived in the third millenium BC, invented marriage, significantly an idea bestowed on the Chinese before succeeding sovereigns invented agriculture, weapons, and porcelain. This is an indication of the importance Chinese tradition gives to marriage as an ingredient of their civilisation, and has resulted in China, until recent times, having one of the most stable forms of family life of any major nation. Ancestry was, as so frequently in primitive societies, originally traced through the maternal line; the Chinese word for 'marry' is *hun-yin*, to take a husband, and at a Chinese wedding feast the bride's relatives are still served first.

Philologists have identified some 400 clan names in Chinese languages and dialects, a version of one of them being given to every Chinese child, along with a personal name, and sometimes a courtesy name in addition. Thus even today a Chinese is conscious of his origin as a member of one of the clans which originally held land and property as communal assets, increasing their value when the men married women from neighbouring clans. Until recently it was forbidden, and is still regarded as ominous for the future, for a man and woman with a similar clan name to marry.

The paternalistic structure of the Chinese family became so deeply imprinted on the Chinese mind that filial duty to the father and paternal ancestors became a way of life—an aim towards perfection which brooked no interference. It was therefore unquestioned that the oldest living male had absolute authority over the lives of every member of the family. He was the mortal representative and spokesman for the family's dead ancestors. After the head of the family and his own offspring came every member related by blood or marriage, including illegitimate children, all in a precise order of precedence. For century after century the elders of the families of the clan met regularly to record the births and marriages of male children.

A woman's place in the Chinese family was tolerable only because of the intense loyalty of men to those acknowledged to be members of the family, to the affectionate nature of a Chinese husband, and the universal love of children. These traits softened what were harsh and rigid laws to safeguard the family structure. A girl could expect to have her betrothal arranged when she was about ten years old, and was not consulted about it. But marriage was deferred until the late teens, and the bridegroom was usually of much the same age as his bride. On marriage the girl was transferred from subjection to her father to that of her husband. If she survived him she became subject to her eldest son. Not for a day of her life was she free from male domination over everything she did.

A Chinese wife was jealously guarded. The ancient custom of binding the feet originated as a precaution against a woman running away. Even though the feet became so badly deformed that a wife could only hobble to work in the rice paddy or to carry out her household tasks, the defects of her contribution to the family's tasks were regarded as well compensated by her restricted life. She accepted the bonds of marriage philosophically: from infancy she had been taught that she had been born a girl because of some sin in a previous existence.

If she bore sons she earned the right to be respected. With increasing age, and after the death of her husband's mother (three and possibly four generations lived in the same dwelling, the existence of several age groups being common because of early marriage and the devoted care of the aged) she could expect to be revered.

Confucius taught a system of ethics rather than preaching a religion. Unlike other great figures who have changed the mind and spirit of mankind, he disclaimed that he had any special contact with the divine, or any mission ordained by God. His culture has had a more profound effect on the people of China than the other widely practised religions of the country, Buddhism and Taoism. The Confucian philosophy was essentially concerned with the mortal life, stressing the duties of men on earth and deprecating attempts to investigate the supernatural. His instructions on universal obligations list five duties: 'those between sovereign and minister, between father and son, between husband and wife, between elder and younger brother, and those belonging to the intercourse of friends'. Thus the concept of family loyalty embraces the whole community, however large it may have become under a titular head. At the same time the nuclear family becomes the heart of the national body.

Confucius's encouragement of ancestor worship included great regard for the centralisation of authority. The Emperor was the father of the State, the eldest man of a clan its father, and the head of each family in it the absolute autocrat. The Confucian insistence on veneration of the father figure, and the symbolism of the family extending to embrace every person in the nation, make it easier to understand the unquestioning adulation of Mao-tse Tung. The first figurehead of communist China exploited the culture which has flourished for more than two thousand years to unify 800 million people, based on the religious dogma that no individual should revolt against family or state, but should resign himself fatalistically to his situation.

Western reports of the segregation of the sexes in village labour barracks, the care of all children in village creches, and the regimentation under commune bureaucrats, suggest that such regimentation must be eventually the source of unrest as unendurable infringements of personal life. But closer examination indicates that the clan system is carefully maintained, at least in the myriad communities of rural workers outside the few large towns. Strict segregation of adolescents and separate meals for unmarried men and women are traditional customs, not a repressive innovation of communist philosophy.

One great non-Christian religion is notable in ignoring national boundaries and politics: Buddhism. The violent assault on Tibet by China was indicative of the fear and respect the communist world feels for this gentle cult, which could not easily be made to support nationalism and the idealism of war. Buddhism also has a profound influence on family life, and not of the kind approved by modern politicians.

Nearly a third of mankind practises Buddhism, which in its classical form holds that mortal existence is evil, though death offers no release because renewed incarnation will start the cycle all over again. Release will come only from *Nirvana*, the loss of individuality in the universal life. Buddha, now worshipped as a god or demi-god by the adherents of many sects, never claimed to be more than a man, and his life, as described in legend and accounts written after his death, is essentially one of a mortal, living a normal life in his youth, and only later aspiring to more than the material world could provide.

Monasticism exerts a strong influence on every man brought up in the Buddhist religion. The almost exclusively male vocation has far greater impact on the masses than the religious orders of Roman Catholicism. It does not necessarily demand life-long vows, and in some countries, notably Burma, a youth becomes a monk as a normal part of his education. He emerges with a regard for self-discipline and has been inculcated with a strict moral code. Sexual indulgence is totally prohibited along with killing, theft, and lying. He is taught to reject excessive eating, drinking of intoxicants, dancing, music, and personal adornment.

Buddhist pessimism about worldly existence and all that it embraces means that direct influence on marriage and family life is less than in most religions. But in its least elaborate forms, Buddhism ensures a quiet contentment in family life. True, there are some taboos as regards touching women, but in marriage there is a real tenderness between husband and wife, warm affection between parents and children, and a high regard for relatives.

Through Buddhism's tolerance, plus the implied dismissal of marriage as of no spiritual importance, the family structure among Buddhist peoples varies according to economic and social influences. Thus change can occur without the breakdown of religious beliefs. The strength which Buddhism confers on the family is the lofty idealism it sows in the mind of every member, man or woman, old or young.

Family life on the Indian sub-continent is based on religious observance as set down in the Hindu holy writ so far as the majority of the population is concerned. The structure is the familiar one of paternal control coupled with protection of family property. The healthy survival of the family line is achieved by strict taboos against marriage of persons too closely related. Cousins are regarded as of the same relationship as brothers and sisters, and marriage between cousins is therefore rare. Dissipation of family property through the introduction of unrelated strains is minimised by the caste system. Men and women must marry within their own caste, and those Hindus who have been converted to other religions still tend to observe the rules of caste. Attempts to abolish caste by secular legislation have not been successful, and an even more formidable problem is of the tens of millions who have no caste status at all, a constant menace to the ancient cultures of family life.

Marriage is regarded as of vital importance to the community and cannot be accepted as a personal matter between a man and a woman.

The force of sexual attraction is therefore something of an obstacle to a desirable union, and its effects have to be curbed. There is the intractable belief, as voiced by the Hindus' beloved poet Rabindranath Tagore, that 'marriage needs must be rescued from the control of the heart, and brought under the province of the intellect; otherwise insoluble problems will keep on arising, for passion considers not the consequences, nor brooks interference by outside judges. For the purpose of marriage spontaneous love is unreliable.' Manu laws enjoined that 'day and night women must be kept in subjection by the male members of the family'. There must be as little contact as possible. A woman is the source of dishonour, because when woman was first created she was given an array of disgraceful emotions: a love of her bed, of her chair, and of ornaments; impure desire, dishonesty, malice, and bad behaviour. Such a creature had to be shunned. But offspring to strengthen and increase the family were needed, so marriage is permissible by the Manu code as a duty, but not for love or sexual satisfaction. The woman's sole purpose was to bear sons, many sons. In order to extend her child-bearing activities to the maximum possible span of her life, child marriage was approved, and became common. Up to 1860 the age of consent was ten, and well into the present century nearly half the girls of the Indian sub-continent were married by the age of fifteen.

The Hindu husband completely owned his wife. He could take another wife, and either divorce or simply isolate the first one, if she was barren, her children failed to survive, or she bore only daughters. If he himself was sterile or impotent he could order his wife to have intercourse with a male relative of his choice, and if she then bore a son, he acknowledged the child as his. With a sensible if rather unexpected regard for native pride the British conquerors of India maintained all the better features of Hindu family laws, and were careful not to interfere too harshly with customs which, while horrifying to the Western mind, helped to maintain the stability of Indian family life. The extreme example of a wife's absolute subjection and fidelity to her husband, Suttee, in which she immolated herself on her husband's funeral pyre, to prove her virtue, was in theory prohibited after 1829, but the practice persisted among Brahmins till the present century, an authenticated case being recorded as late as 1936.

Ostensibly the complete subjection of women and the unquestioned dominance of men are now part of past Indian history. In 1942 a committee meticulously made a careful examination of the Hindu cultural and social patterns, and as a result in 1956 a new code was written, notable features of which were the abolition of polygamy and the provision of equal rights for women as regards succession and inheritance. But in the minds of millions of men—and, for that matter, women—the marriage and family customs which have prevailed since the 6th century BC cannot be abandoned without angering the divinities of their religion.

For the maintenance of a traditional social, cultural and economic way of life, strong enough to withstand appalling problems of poverty, hunger, and personal injustice, the Hindu policy on marriage and family has proved itself obstinately hostile to compromise and change. It has the paradoxical result that a cult with an earthy veneration of sex and fertility also demands that erotic love shall have no part in marriage. As a consequence sexual pleasure is set apart from marriage, and is then given a degree of importance almost as great. Eroticism is both an art and a science to Hindus. A word most closely approximating to 'joy' is *mithuna*, which is also the word for sexual intercourse.

To the Hindu, the divine order of life was to separate the family from the physical passions which surge through human beings. The ideal for the few might be asceticism and chastity, with rejection of both family and sex in mortal life. For the mass of people the practical way to protect the family and assuage the sex hunger was to obey the religious taboos and keep family considerations and sexual desire apart. No one who ponders on the efforts of other civilisations and religions to unite erotic love with the family structure can dismiss the Hindu attitude as completely wrong, except for one thing: the price which both marriage customs and sexual satisfaction demands from women. With education, emancipation, and contact with the West it is difficult to believe that the age-old imbalance of the privileges and duties of Hindu men and women will survive unaltered. The changing attitudes already occurring among the wealthier urban families are still of minimal importance in a nation of 500 million people, most living in abject poverty and wary of innovation. But the seeds have been sown. It remains to be seen whether a family system 'as old as mankind' will give way to the cult of equality for all men and all women. Most Indians, when challenged, will deny the possibility.

Islam, the newest of the world religions, has modified marriage and family life among nations stretching from West Africa to Malaysia. The Moslem acceptance of sexual intercourse between men and women as normal and desirable has not, however, resulted in a high regard for women. Their status is subordinate in the extremely comprehensive rules provided in the Koran. Marriage is essentially for the begetting of offspring, though it is a civil ceremony, thus obviating any suggestion of permanence of the union under divine law. Divorce is simple for a man (and virtually impossible for a woman unless Western influences have penetrated the country concerned). The Koran for centuries was interpreted as allowing a man four wives, plus concubines, though this is now questioned. Personal slaves are allowed, but a female slave who is taken as a concubine can expect her child to inherit the father's property on equal terms with the offspring of the wife.

The desire to ensure the stability of the male line is indicated in Islamic inheritance laws : males must benefit by twice the value of the family assets as those bequeathed to the females and the testator cannot will away more than a third of his estate to non-members of his family.

The notable feature common to all types of family structure in the countries of the non-Christian world is the deep and unquestioning respect held for kinship, and the comparatively minor regard for the emotional factors of affection between husband and wife. Personal feelings must be subordinated to the benefit of the majority. The people of the West have steadily rejected the claims of kinship since a predominantly urban civilisation gave the majority the means of livelihood outside the family enterprise or household, and the change of attitude is accompanied by a decline in the importance of the large family embracing many relatives. In the Middle and Near East, and in Asia, the old system is now being attacked. It is probably so strongly established that no major change in the foreseeable future will occur, and the West, assailed by doubts about the quality of life based on acquisition and self-interest, may well look to cultures hitherto regarded as quaint or backward in order to regain a sense of identity in an over-populated environment of anonymous persons controlled by a faceless bureaucracy. If so, the religions of the East could provide the pattern—a generous repayment in return for the materialistic benefits derived from the West.

Bibliography for this chapter is on pp176-7.

8 *Experimental Family Structures Today*

A scrutiny of the cultural patterns which mankind has devised and followed over almost half a million years provides evidence of similarity more frequently than difference. The objects of creating a personally satisfying existence as well as an entity of benefit to the community as a whole have not greatly changed. The family has always been in a state of transition; it has never been permanently weakened. If there is a noteworthy alteration in the family structure today it is in the division between the pattern of marital partnership and the larger, more conventional, unit of ancestors, descendants and kin. Hasty judgement and unfounded criticism of current and imminent trends in marriage as inimical to the survival of the family are unwarranted. Continuous experiment in types of male-female union, the nucleus of the family structure, is as noteworthy a feature of mankind's history as the resilience of the family is its imperishable asset.

It could be claimed that too rigid a culture of marriage customs and laws, perpetuating a system which frequently created a wretched and sometimes unbearable situation for the individual, can be the greatest menace to the family and therefore to the social health of the community, the nation, and humanity at large. If this be so, then current contemporary experimentation in new forms of sexual union, as practised in California and the 'advanced' urban classes of Western Europe, so far from imposing a death sentence on the family, will give it renewed strength in the challenge it doubtless faces from soulless and materialistic State control. The family will not change its fundamental structure and will not decline in social importance. But marriage is clearly moving towards a period of experiment, wherein the underlying motive for change is devotion to the happiness of the individual. Marriage as we have practised it therefore may not always be an ingredient of family life, and the traditional form of permanent monogamy may well fall away to become just one of a number of marital patterns.

A minority of married couples, admittedly quite a small one, already regards marriage as an arrangement hopefully to last for a period of years, but not necessarily for a lifetime. Rationalisation of this evidently growing trend would be to dignify serial marriage with social and official tolerance, and eventually approval. First might come trial marriage, advocated two generations ago as a means of decreasing the risks of lifelong misery or costly and often harrowing legal action should the relationship break down. Many young people are, of course, already practising a form of trial marriage with extra-marital sex.

More than half the live first births to British women under twenty years of age occur within eight months of marriage. Most of the couples were intending to marry. Since most couples indulging in pre-marital sex can learn about methods of avoiding conception they cannot be castigated as promiscuous for they have their own codes of moral behaviour which include mutual fidelity. The girl who 'sleeps around' with mere acquaintances is strongly criticised in most young social groups, and the boy is expected to become the exclusive sexual partner of his selected girl.

This is trial marriage in all but strictly legal or religious terms. In a future culture the accent on romantic impulses and sexual activity strictly confined to the two persons concerned might give it an old-fashioned, even reactionary, image. Its close identity with the lifelong monogamous relationships of the past (the trial husband and wife presumably hope to convert their partnership to a permanent union if they continue to find it satisfactory) makes it the least revolutionary of current prophecies of marriage patterns in the twenty-first century. The idea of trial marriage originated in the first half of the twentieth century, not as a substitute for the then established style of marriage, but as a safeguard against the latter's subsequent breakdown. The new version could be a replacement of what to many young people seems to be a potentially unsuccessful form of sexual union. Trial marriage would have to embody provisions for its temporary nature so as to facilitate a simple dissolution later, and one can envisage stipulations by the State against the birth of children unless the temporary union was confirmed as a permanent development. Maximum duration for a trial marriage might be fixed at ten years, with permission for formal dissolution at any time after, say, three years. At the end of the ten-year period the couple would either separate or enter into a main marriage which would be the recognised union as regards inheritances and other material factors. This main marriage might with advantage be made comparatively difficult, with physical and psychological checks as to the couple's suitability to enter into a contract of direct interest to society. The goal of an approved main marriage might be to rear children, to further some social, business, professional or artistic activity, or for frankly hedonistic reasons. The aim and purpose would have to be stated, and medical tests would confirm or reject the validity of the claims. None need be regarded as more desirable than the others from a social viewpoint.

In view of the over-population problem it might be expected that the couple authorised to start a family would be given a directive on the number of children and how to space the births. In return for acquiescence to State supervision of the family's size the parents could be rewarded with special benefits in maternity grants, tax concessions, child allowances, housing, and job security.

A main marriage, designedly sterile, would not be regarded as anti-social. Husband-and-wife teams would be extremely valuable to society and industry. The present wastage of public money and personal energy with many thousands of young women obtaining degrees in the sciences, and many more thousands acquiring industrial and business skills in a brief period of employment, is due for change.[1] Skilled persons living in a childless main marriage would almost inevitably become the leaders in every branch of a nation's life. In the lower echelons of the social structure they would be highly mobile, easily transferred for the operations of world-wide commercial organisations and transport services, and to industrial and constructional projects. They would form the personnel in international government agencies, in the sciences dealing with ecology, exploration, and new areas of food production. The cream of this section of society would work as a two-person team with a single-minded determination to attain a desired goal. In politics, international finance, and the pure sciences their freedom from ties of family and competing interests would allow a sense of vocation to flourish. It might well become a normal thing for a husband and wife to represent a Parliamentary constituency jointly. Industrial and commercial concerns engaged in highly technical and competitive business with strong security considerations, which already vet wives of senior executives, would offer joint appointments for husbands and wives who were not merely 'safe' but were both of positive value to the organisation.

The final marriage partnership would normally be undertaken in the late fifties and sixties. This would be at a time when the main marriage had lasted about twenty years—the duration which produced a high incidence of divorce under the English divorce laws prior to 1971, and accounting for nearly a fifth of all divorce cases.[2] There would, of course, be nothing to prevent a couple confirming the existing partnership, and one may assume that the majority of middle-aged couples, set in their ways, experienced in making mutual adjustments, and enjoying a union which had become a satisfying habit, would do so. For the minority who desired change a new marriage would abolish the dull hopelessness which undoubtedly many middle-aged couples face with quiet resignation after twenty years of marriage. The inevitable changes in personal outlook, emotion, and in economic conditions at this stage are probably as profound as those of puberty and early adult life. Even if the age for retirement does not markedly drop some measure of demotion in employment and the consequent decrease in income will become usual. The changes will not be solely economic. Those main marriages which have produced offspring will revert to two-person families. The children will have grown up and moved to independent status as employed persons or taken over by the State for further education away from home. Emotional demands by parents on these young adults will be taboo under the already accepted standards of the older generation leaving the succeeding one to mould its own life. Yet these parents will not be resigned to sit back placidly in the evening of their lives fatalistically awaiting death. They will be men and women with some twenty years of active life ahead of them. Both husband and wife will need new incentives and interests. Sexual urges may be sublimated by devising new ways to gain power and wealth or by taking up hobbies, which are a solution so long as the ideas of both are compatible and are accompanied by the survival or even some rejuvenation of their sexual interest in one another. If not, then from their own point of view, such couples will be told by the doctors and marriage guidance counsellors of the future that it might be better to separate and form new unions—the final serial marriage.

This final marriage pattern might be a calculated design for living, embarked on after careful discussion and a trial period of life together to see if it would work, and thus have very little romance about it. Given this forethought and preparation the marriages could develop into placid, companionable partnerships eventually reminiscent of the Darby and Joan image of the past. But some older people can be expected to choose the group marriage idea as practised by twenty-first century young people in their colleges and youth communes. It is worth recalling that in the 1960s the practice of temporarily exchanging partners was called 'wife swapping' among the younger age groups and 'mate swapping' by those in their forties and fifties. In the former group the practice was in reality crude promiscuity of a very old-fashioned type: the men regarded women as sex toys and their own wives as inferiors who had to do what they were told. But the older age groups, describing the practice as mate swapping, had an unexpected and quite modernistic regard for sex equality. The exchange of sexual partners had to be mutually agreeable, and the tendency was for these changes not to be for one night, but for a defined period.

Mate swapping in the twentieth century appeared to have taboos on any permanence. The convention was never to repeat a partnership at the next exchange ceremony. This was, in effect, group marriage. It would be far more convenient, and less socially destructive, if middle aged people, sophisticated and tolerant about sex, considered whether they could find ten or a dozen married couples who could get on as a social group, co-operating on the practical routines of meals, dwelling place, recreation, and cultural interests, and not possessive sexually, forming a group household. Not least of the advantages would be the economies possible in the share of housework, residence, cars, and so on. The final serial marriage might therefore develop, either spontaneously or by intent and discussion, into a group marriage.

Serial marriage on a wide scale will erode romantic theories about everyone being allotted one perfect partner, and one only, by some machination of Fate. More people will accept, as millions have always known, that genuine affection can be felt at successive periods of life for more than one beloved person. This is at present a permissible emotion so long as bereavement or separation end the earlier partnership. But sexual attraction towards more than one person simultaneously is invariably regarded as a source of tragedy or evidence of sinfulness. Loving one person is a virtue, loving two a vice. Yet there are no valid arguments to prove that a man having several wives, or for that matter a woman having several husbands, is immoral and decadent. Polygamy has never been a subject of serious controversy in Britain since the arrival of Christianity, though it may soon occur if communities of people of Asian origin within the larger industrial towns continue to be isolated and therefore encouraged to create an environment and culture reminiscent of the ancestral birthplace. Freedom of religious belief might be said to include freedom to practise the forms of marriage permitted by some religions.

The problem of polygamy had to be faced in the United States after the founding of the Church of Jesus Christ of Latter-Day Saints (Mormons) in 1830. Until the US Government stipulated that the practice of polygamy would have to be abandoned in return for admission of Utah as a state of the Union the legal position of Mormons with more than one wife, and living in Missouri, Ohio, and Illinois, where there were thousands of converts, presented a tricky problem in that the Constitution provided that 'Congress shall make no law respecting an establishment of religion or prohibiting the free exercise thereof'.

During the hearing of a classic case in which a Mormon named Cleveland had moved across a state boundary with his wives and was thereupon charged with contravening the Mann

Act (which made it an offence to move with any woman or girl across a state boundary for the purpose of prostitution or debauchery or for any immoral purpose), Chief Justice Waite described marriage as a social institution (thereby implying that its social implications were more important than its religious status) and this the law was entitled to protect. A second judge considered that polygamy was a notorious example of promiscuity, but a third observed that 'even when marriage occurs in a form of which we disapprove it is not to be equated with prostitution or debauchery'. This minority view did not save Cleveland, and he was found guilty. Mormons were naturally indignant, and many Americans with a deep veneration for the Constitution were disturbed at what they considered a restriction on a citizen's birthright of freedom of religious belief.

The controversy over legalised polygamy disappeared with the termination of the Mormons' approval of it. Since then various sects have tacitly permitted forms of polygamy for their self-appointed leaders who have lived with 'angels', 'apostles' and similar euphemisms for concubinage. Otherwise America, like the rest of the white nations, has settled for the convenience of mistresses and serial polygamy by periodic divorce and re-marriage. Polygamy was declared illegal in the USA in 1890.

The State's disapproval of polygamy could easily be modified if the government considered it desirable. Morality would then be adjusted to comply. When the Anabaptists wished to increase the political power of the theocratic state which they founded at Munster in 1533 and to develop a population large enough to resist the Protestant princes of Germany, it was proclaimed that the true Christian had more than one wife (the main result of this advice was a period of sexual licence). In a similar move to increase the birth rate, in 1650 the imperial city of Nuremburg announced that every man should be allowed to marry two women in order to restore a population decimated by the Thirty Years' War. It is possible to visualise some catastrophe of genocide in a future global war or massive casualties in a natural disaster which would encourage the surviving nations to authorise polygamy as the simplest and obvious way to replace lost populations.

Bigamy, the only form of polygamy practised in Britain, is rare, or at least rarely discovered.[3] Apart from the period of abnormal conditions in periods of modern wars the number of offences of bigamy is fairly steady at about 250 per year, if offences in a real sense they are. Transgression of religious law can hardly be cited when the bigamist goes to a registrar's office. He offends technically by giving fraudulent details of his personal status and is a nuisance in that he contributes to inaccuracies in the State records, but so do those who give an incorrect age or address. By the standards of Christian morality the bigamist is an adulterer, but that is hardly a role now likely to ostracise him socially, and anyway adultery is not a crime.

It can be seen that in a society which is predominantly sceptical of religious law, bigamy practised with complete honesty and openness might quite easily become acceptable to the State, and it may be added, to many marriage partners who would acquiesce to the existence or even the presence of a second partner of the same sex in preference to being deserted. Some form of simultaneous polygamy, in place of the present prevalence of serial monogamy or the wife-and-mistress and husband-and-lover households, also seems feasible in the future where communities or nations have a considerable difference in sex ratios. By the year 2001 projections by the Government Statistical Service suggests that the United Kingdom population will have a surplus of 800,000 females. In the first-marriage ages of 20-24, however, men will be a trifle more numerous than women, so monogamy, other marriage customs apart, will be the easiest way of forming marital unions in these age groups. The preponderance of men over women will continue through the age groups up to 44; thereafter the surplus of women over men will grow larger. It is therefore among the middle-aged that polygamy might become attractive.

Historically polygamy has been practised primarily in primitive societies for economic considerations: the advantages of having several wives to work, prepare food, and to symbolise wealth and power. Socially, in more civilised communities, it was a method of having many sons to continue and increase the family line. None of these factors is of great import today, although the probable decline in major differences in rewards for work for the individual, and the increasing benefits in employment for women, would enable families of one man and several women to enjoy materialistic advantages greater than those of monogamous families.

Polyandry, with one woman having more than one husband, was, according to legend plus some fairly reliable evidence, prevalent in Britain before the Roman occupation. It is a feature of a matriarchical society and matrilinear descent, with the husbands frequently brothers. It cannot be dismissed as an improbable development if ardent feminism continues to spread. Polyandry is proof of woman's mastery over the male, and might make a strong appeal to future cohorts of the women's liberation movement as a common sense alternative to absolute rejection of the male as a sexual companion, colleague, or friend.

In suggesting polygamy as a possibility for the imminent future one must bear in mind that, if it is to be a middle-of-life custom, those embarking on it will have been the young people of the permissive society of the 1960s and 70s. They will be sexual and social sophisticates to whom yet another experiment could be attractive. When these middle-aged people reach old age, but with many years of life before them, still other forms of companionate living may appeal. The individual's problem of living rather than existing for the last two or three decades of human life will be in urgent need of a practical solution. So far, old age has been generalised as an economic problem of providing adequate pensions and housing, with a leavening of discussion about medical treatment of the comparatively small percentage who suffer from major disease. Too little has been said about the emotional situation of the ordinary man and woman of sixty years plus, who is not poverty-stricken, inadequately housed, or mentally or physically ill. By sheer weight of their increasing numbers these people will inevitably find themselves coming into the social limelight. Thirteen million people in Britain and 42 million in the United States now between 45 and 64 will be the pensioners of the closing years of the twentieth century. Their mode of existence will be of enormous influence on the social structure of the nation.

Two roads are open: absorption of these 'senior citizens' in their families, as was the practice throughout the world in the past and still prevails beyond the borders of the heavily in-dustrialised Western nations; or an increasing segregation voluntarily adopted by the old people themselves. The former trend is unlikely. Whatever changes occur in the family the isolation of the generations can be expected to continue. Exist-ing housing, which will have to last for generations ahead, is almost entirely designed solely for the parents-children family unit, with no room for additional members. In most modern marriages one or both of the partners will regard the housing and feeding of a parent or parents as a burden rather than a privilege. The desire for identification and independence is now deeply implanted among people of all ages—and this desire for freedom from family or social chains is really for divisions among the generations. Segregation is acceptable to young, middle aged, and old, whatever protests and denials they may feel they ought to make.

The attitude that the onset of retirement age marks a time when a new routine of living should begin has already become widespread. New interests are deliberately sought, and the old home is abandoned. Communities are growing in which the majority of residents are of pension age, and as they move in the younger people plan to move out. Lack of space and re-strictions on building developments in Britain necessitate a compromise by the aged in more or less taking over an existing community instead of creating a tailor-made one. In the long run the State would find a better bargain, and the elderly would find a more congenial way of life, if the American system of building completely new 'senior citizen' communities could be adopted. By 1971 there were dozens of these communities in the USA, many of a size large enough to be called towns, and equipped with the facilities enjoyed by people no longer physically active.

Parallel with this geographical identification of the subculture of the elderly are the moves to combine in social organisations, primarily designed to watch over the interests of members, but automatically prepared to compete with other age groups for a slice of the national welfare cake and the national wealth.

In the United Kingdom such welfare organisations as the British Association of Retired Persons, Cruse, and the National Old People's Welfare Council, and the Association of Retired Persons, and the National Council of Senior Citizens in the USA, can now exert strong political influence and can mould conventions and customs to improve both the lives— and as important, the image—of the elderly. How the elderly organise the twenty or thirty years of existence many of them can expect to enjoy (or endure) will have a profound effect on the general culture.

They will see to it that they continue to enjoy at least a measure of the benefits of companionship and affection which a human being always needs. For the majority, perhaps, there is no problem for a greater part of their lives in retirement: the marriage partner is alive. But in Britain today nearly 2 million widows and about 600,000 widowers over sixty-four have a ceaseless battle against loneliness. In the United States the number of widows is 6 million, and widowers $1\frac{1}{2}$ million.

These figures will inevitably continue to increase for the rest of the century. Projections forecast that there will be 4.6 million men and 6.5 million women over the age of sixty in the Britain of 1981, 9.6 million men and 13.9 million women in the USA in 1980. With the retention of the usual retirement age of sixty-five for men and sixty for women 16.5 per cent of the population of the United Kingdom will then have finished their lifetime of work.

Frankness about sexual matters has not hitherto been extended to the needs and appetites of older people. The forebodings about future sexual potency among men, and the fear of declining sexual enjoyment among women, is largely a relic of the juvenile belief that one's parents could not possibly enjoy sex, and this has been wildly exaggerated by society's accent on the sexuality of youth in the second half of the twentieth century. Sexuality is of course not such an irrepressible driving force as the years go by, but among married couples who have been sexually well matched the sex drive can survive well into the seventh and even the eighth decade of life.

Questionnaires circulated over a ten-year period by Duke University, California, to aged men indicated that they had experienced little change in their sex interest when they were in their late seventies, and although fewer women maintained interest both sexes showed that if their sexual lives had been adjusted and enjoyed in early life it was maintained with only a slight decrease in activity. The death of the marital partner did, of course, enforce termination of sexual activity for most of the septuagenarians—unless they could remarry. As well as these widowed men and women there are large numbers of divorced persons of middle age and over. Prior to 1971 nearly a fifth of the people divorced in Britain had been married for twenty years and more, involving about 20,000 persons aged 40-plus in an average year. It is reasonable to surmise that one partner in each of these dissolved marriages had no lover or new marriage partner in view at the time of the court hearing, and in fact only about 112 divorced women and 188 divorced men (of all ages) per thousand do in fact remarry.

For the personal happiness of these people, and for the direct benefit of the State in maintaining acceptable standards of living for the elderly, particularly as regards the old adage that 'two can live as cheaply as one', which, if not arithmetically true, has some validity for a couple cohabiting in one living unit, a final marriage in the last decades of life would be an acceptable and often welcome event. Such marriages would, of course, be mainly for the purpose of companionship, economy, and social advantage. The last factor is important because modern society operates on the assumption that an adult is one of a duo. The loner is regarded suspiciously, compassionately, or with hardly concealed annoyance. Whatever the underlying reaction, he or she is different, a semi-outcast. This sense of being unwanted and superfluous fills the psychiatric wards and clinics, and drives the old to utter despair. The rates for suicide and self-inflicted injury for men aged 45-64 are more than double those for men of 15-34, and more than treble for women in the same age groups. Re-marriage in later life as an accepted custom would be a valuable yet simple means of giving meaning to life and pleasure in living it. The State could save itself much expensive direct care, and would encourage the elderly to re-create a way of life which was the pattern of their adult existence by a new marriage, if they did not penalise the pensioner by paying less to a man and wife than to a widower and widow.

A greater measure of tolerance towards unions which have no claim to strengthen the family structure, to produce offspring, or to maintain the status of matrimony set down in religious and temporal law, could be extended to unions at present regarded as perverted, but which do in fact already exist in various kinds of subterfuge. It therefore seems within the bounds of probability that in some 'advanced' countries formal unions of two persons of the same sex will be socially acceptable and given a degree of legality so that such privileges as tax allowances and married persons' pensions will apply in the same manner as for heterosexual unions. The recognition among most Western nations, and in many other countries emulating the American-European design for civilisation, that many men and women marry only for sexual satisfaction and companionship, without any intention of creating a family by having offspring, has encouraged suggestions that homosexual marriages, in which the motives of the two persons concerned would be almost exactly the same as in deliberately childless male-female unions based solely on mutual attraction, would be of psychological and even social benefit to innumerable sexual inverts.

The *de facto* homosexual marriage is already in existence and has been for centuries. Social opprobrium and legal vetoes have necessitated such unions being clandestine, or disguised in some other kind of relationship. The strain of some degree of pretence or of ceaseless precautions to ensure that legal penalties are avoided has in the past resulted in many male homosexual unions being ephemeral and riddled with violent jealousies, plus the invidious repercussions of blackmail, male prostitution, and promiscuous activities in order to find a partner. The long-established tolerance of homosexuality in Scandinavia (and in Germany prior to the 'night of the long knives' in the formative phase of Nazism), the legalisation of homosexual practices between consenting adults in Britain, and the—perhaps involuntary—tolerance now accorded to minority groups in the USA, are apparently a preface to eventual recognition of homosexual unions as acceptable examples of human sexual activity. With a chink made in the armour of established convention it seems certain that the militancy of homosexuals in the closing years of the twentieth century will be directed towards attaining full social and legal recognition for themselves and their way of life.

The Kinsey surveys in the USA remain among the most reliable sources of information on the proportion of homosexuals in a modern multi-racial and industrial society. These indicated that 10 per cent of men and 4 per cent of women live through periods of varying duration of exclusive homosexuality. Many of these people go through a disturbing emotional period in adolescence or during some later crisis in their lives, and a few may be temporarily swayed by homosexual seduction. The figures for temporary homosexuality are not important so far as the pattern of marriage and family life is concerned. Of greater significance is Kinsey's finding that in the USA 4 per cent of males and 2 per cent of females were totally homosexual all their lives. In Britain a similar estimate would mean that there are more than one million male and about 600,000 female homosexuals of all ages. A young permanent homosexual has so far faced a future in which he or she can quietly partner someone of like emotions in a *de facto* marriage; create a deceptive situation by formally marrying a homosexual of the opposite sex, with both agreeing to go their own emotional ways; or attempt the near-impossible of seeking happiness and emotional satisfaction in a faithfully observed heterosexual marriage. The first has always been the wisest policy and is now feasible in the sectionalised groupings of the community in large cities. The second is restricted to those wealthy and sophisticated enough to find compliant partners and to be able to organise their double lives with unremitting concern for secrecy and deception. The third procedure, forced in particular on the middle classes by lack of wealth and their rigid conventions about correct social living, is redolent of private tragedy, not least for the normally sexed victim who is defrauded into what he or she believes to be marriage with a genuinely heterosexual partner.

In Britain further relaxation of legal strictures, which will lessen the need for furtiveness, appears to be reasonably certain. The Sexual Law Reform Society, under the chairmanship of Dr John Robinson, Dean of Trinity College, Cambridge (previously Bishop of Woolwich), has proposed revisions of British law, virtually abolishing any distinct category of crime as regards sexual offences, except for those against children, affronts to public decency, and sexual activities involving coercion. The laws of England referring to male homosexual practices (modified in 1967 as the result of the

Wolfenden report) came into force as a result of the Offences against the Person Act of 1861; they omitted any reference to lesbianism, allegedly because of the Home Secretary's anxiety to avoid bringing such a delicate subject to the attention of Queen Victoria. As a result lesbianism in Britain was (and has remained) a completely lawful activity—an unusual example of sex inequality.

Whatever general recommendations on sexual offences the reformers make, actual changes to the law will have then to be studied by the Criminal Law Revision Committee, and this body was thought unlikely to make a report until late in the 1970s. But the Law Commission has already commenced studies of the factors in civil law which concern the legal status of people who biologically are of one sex but psychologically of the opposite one, as well as transexuals whose sex is uncertain. Some lawyers believe that the status of these people in civil law is more important than the potential dangers they may run from the operations of criminal law. Any concessions as regards inheritance, marital status, and other identifications by sex would clearly pave the way for eventual recognition of sexual relationships hitherto regarded as abnormal or illicit.

The case against condoning and eventually approving freely adopted homosexual unions is that they are perverted distortions of the natural sexual motivation designed by nature for reproducing the species; that they therefore offend against natural law as well as established moral, social and religious codes; that their sterility makes them worthless to society in general and the families directly concerned in particular; that tolerance of homosexuality is historically a symptom of national decadence.

Arguments against these criticisms are that if homosexuality is freakish then nature herself is responsible for the existence of a vast number of distorted creatures, both human and animal, and the emotional switch involved does not inhibit their efficient functioning; that distaste for practices which cannot have the fertile outcome of similar practices on a heterosexual level assumes that the sexual drive is biologically and psychologically only for reproduction of the species—a theory which cannot be of any influence on animals and is rejected by human beings for most of their lives. Sexual inversion obviously infringes the moral laws which emerge from religious belief and social custom, but objectively this distaste can be regarded as originally contrived by the majority as an oppression of a minority. The sterility of homosexual unions is a valid criticism only if marriage is regarded as primarily the concern of society at large and has nothing to do with the contentment of the persons who go into a sexual partnership. In this the historical background is the important factor, as it is with regard to changes in modern marriage patterns. The charge that a homosexual union is anti-social could be as strongly made about deliberately childless heterosexual unions, and quite often is in countries where an expanding population appears desirable.

Homosexuality as a symptom of national decadence has almost as much evidence to refute the charge as to support it. The Persian, Greek, and Roman empires permitted, and sometimes encouraged, homosexuality throughout their development and ascendancy, and though it became more prevalent, along with sexual excesses and aberrations of all kinds, in their decline, homosexuality can hardly be regarded as the main cause of the downfall and defeat of these civilisations. In England relaxation of traditional religious disciplines as a sequel to the Reformation resulted in widespread homosexuality, but no one could dismiss the England of Elizabeth I as decadent: the robust flowering of literature and science, and the expansion of national power and prestige through exploration and war have hardly been excelled in this or any other country before or since as examples of a nation's strength and energy.

If antipathy to the male homosexual will prevent complete social recognition for a long time ahead, a change of attitude

K

may well be accelerated by the propaganda of lesbians. The belief of Simone de Beauvoir that lesbianism is a reaction against the inferior position allocated to women in all cultures cannot be considered as having any scientific basis, but it has become a favoured claim in the women's liberation movements, sometimes to the fury of adherents who would prefer a respectable image. Lesbianism does not suffer from suspicion and distaste on the part of the public as does male homosexuality. It has never provided sensational scandals in court hearings (except in those rare instances when a female invert has masqueraded as a male and gone through a marriage ceremony with a woman in the presence of an unsuspecting priest or registrar). Tolerance, ignorance, or sheer disbelief have tended to clothe lesbianism in an aura of romanticism quite unknown in the majority's attitude to male sexual inversion. Lesbians have in the past few years organised themselves with great efficiency. The nation-wide lesbian organisation in the USA runs chapters in the large cities from a headquarters with a full-time staff, including a public relations officer, and has many thousands of members who make no secret of their type of sexuality. London has its own lesbian societies, clubs, pubs, and quietly-run projects such as holidays, job opportunities, and legal and medical advisory services. In Amsterdam, regarded as the world headquarters for advancing the rights of lesbians, a club with lecture hall, restaurant, library and recreation rooms is run for lesbians as well as male homosexuals, with the approval, and in many directions actual co-operation, of the police and urban authorities.

The American enthusiasm for public demonstrations has resulted in the US homosexual appearing to have moved farther towards obtaining his own niche in society than in fact he has as compared with the tolerance in Europe. But the American publicity campaign acts as a world wide propaganda machine. The Gay Liberation Front holds parades and demonstrations, with Gay Pride Weeks designed to influence the public on a national scale.

American homosexuals have entered city halls and asked for a marriage licence, causing harassed clerks to check up that state laws did clearly and precisely insist on two sexes for marriage. A religious body in California called the Metropolitan Community Church regularly conducts weddings between homosexuals, using the words of the marriage service of the Episcopal church.[4] In a published discussion the Rev Robert Weeks, an Episcopal clergyman with a well known church in Manhattan, New York, mentioned a man who had been 'married' to another homosexual for fifteen years: 'Both are very happy and much in love. They asked me to bless their marriage and I am going to do it'.

A small, but so far as the individual is concerned, an important change in marriage laws will concern persons who have undergone a 'sex change'. True hermaphroditism in human beings and the higher animals appears to be non-existent, or so rare that from a social viewpoint it can be ignored. Abnormal hermaphroditism with secondary sex characteristics different from the exterior sexual features is, however, common enough to rank as a problem in a society where the rights of the individual are theoretically of paramount importance. With the acceptance of the medical profession that such a condition can be, and needs to be, tackled by surgery or hormone treatment, the number of persons who have undergone sex changes is now considerable. One estimate of the number now living in Britain is 200, mostly persons registered at birth as males who now live as females.[5]

Hitherto these people have lived their new lives, in which the mental as well as the physical characteristics of sex have been modified, as a form of lie. Their birth certificates remain unchanged, describing them as of the sex identified at their birth. Their passports record their new sex. For some time at least their State registration in National Insurance records ignored their biological change, and if they marry someone of

the sex opposite to that of their new sex the union is in danger
of being declared void. An organisation of sex-changed persons now exists to campaign for such persons to have the right
to marry as individuals of their post-treatment sex.

Another form of relationship hitherto regarded as illegal
and immoral which has been cited as due for future legal
respectability is incest. A research organisation in Middle-
town, Connecticut, called the Institute for the Future, en-
deavours to plot social life ahead by reducing guesswork to
scientific forecasting with the aid of computers digesting the
views of experts. In the early nineteen-seventies they were
forecasting changes and developments up to 2025. On the
cultural side the Institute believes that among the taboos due
to disappear is that against incest.

Sexual contacts between persons of the same family line
have not always been regarded as evil. The Egyptian dynastic
culture is an example. The moral laws imposed by world
religions have often been varied as regards the prohibited and
permissible degrees of relationship, and in modern times there
has sometimes been a clash of attitudes between State and
Church over who may or may not marry.

Eugenically an incestuous union which may produce de-
fective offspring is obviously undesirable, even though animal
breeders regularly take a more optimistic view, practically
every domesticated species being deliberately subjected to in-
breeding for the improvement of the stock.

That incest is quite prevalent as a furtive and temporary
activity is undeniable. Parent-child sexual relationships would
surely remain ethically and morally disgusting however
tolerant society becomes. They always suggest the presence
of seduction by the old of the innocent young. The brother-
sister union is apparently the form the American prophets
envisage, and in this regard a sign of the times was the proposal introduced in the Danish Parliament in 1969 to legalise
the marriage of a brother and sister. It went no farther than
laying a Bill before the legislature, but never before in the

Christian era would such a proposal have seen the light of day. In English law on incest, brother and sister also mean half-brother and half-sister, when only one parent is common to each. In the modern prevalence of divorce and re-marriage, with a series of family households separated and isolated from one another, accidental contacts between half-siblings, quite unaware of their biological parentage, is quite likely, and the possibility of such unions is increased by the prevalence of extra-marital liaisons concealed by the married woman concerned. A typical case came before the Hampshire Assizes in June 1971. A young married couple were charged with making a false declaration for contracting a marriage and with incest. The fact that they were the children of one mother was quite unknown to them until the mother revealed it. All the judge could do was to put the couple on probation and make an order that they were immediately to cease having sexual intercourse with one another. He was compassionate enough to tell them not to go away with any sense of serious guilt.

Apart from the possibility of incestuous unions resulting from concealed facts or perjured details at registration of birth, there are the problems for groups of children growing up as a family who are not blood-related even though socially they come to regard themselves as brothers and sisters, whereas in fact one group are the offspring of a mother and the other of a father in previous marital unions, who then marry one another and possibly produce a third group half-related to each of the other groups. In this complicated modern family relationship marriage between half-siblings and so-called siblings would not be incestuous in some instances but would be in others. One cannot see how youths and girls could instinctively discriminate in their sexual desires, particularly when it is borne in mind that 'instinct' will not provide a ruling for the avoidance of incestuous attraction. Marriage between siblings, half-siblings or foster-siblings would be of no direct concern to the State any more than marriages of homosexuals so long as the family unit thus created was born and died during the adult life of the couple involved. To safeguard the racial future incestuous marriage would have to be deliberately infertile, by enforced contraception, sterilisation, or abortion.

State control of this kind would necessarily be complemented by increasing intervention in these marriages yielding offspring. Apart from the need to control the quality and quantity of the renewing generation, the national executive will be compelled to keep pace with the advances of science in regulating conception, pregnancy, and birth.

Notes and Bibliography for this chapter are on pp 177-8

9 *Science as the Family's Dictator*

In advanced Western societies about 12 per cent of marriages are sterile. In Britain this means that there are always about a million couples who will remain involuntarily childless unless there is some kind of extraneous aid to the natural processes of conception. This may be comparatively simple in the majority of cases, because only a very small percentage of adult men and women are completely sterile except as the result of surgical operation, injury, or major disease. Sub-fertility in one marriage partner may not do more than make conception difficult. If both partners are sub-fertile then the likelihood of natural conception becomes remote. In childless unions statistics indicate that the man is five times more likely to be infertile than the woman, though the reason is often due to psychological disturbance, rather than physical disability.

The male's defects are not usually concerned with his semen output. About 300 million sperms are released in each act of intercourse, and this release will occur anything from 6,000 to 15,000 times in a man's life. During the Nazi breeding experiments with members of the SS, the stud males were allegedly mated twice a week. A greater frequency was said to impair their fertility. With the need for only one sperm out of 300 million to survive and reach the egg it can be seen that failure on the part of the male to give his sperm a chance to do so is the more usual masculine defect. As many as 6 per cent of wives attending infertility clinics have been found to be virgins. Impotence is far more common than vanity allows the average male to admit. In women there may be harmful bacteria in the secretions of the sexual organs, deficiency in the alkaline mucus essential for the journey of the sperm, blockage of the fallopian tubes, or spasm of the vaginal muscles through frigidity. None of these male and female defects is now beyond successful treatment.

This medical probing into the most intimate and delicate of marital relationships will undoubtedly become more general both as a means of ensuring desired conception and in new and more reliable techniques to prevent it when children are undesired. One may envisage a future where medical checks on the fertility of a man and woman contemplating marriage will be a routine procedure, with periodic investigations throughout the fertile period of married life. In some regimented society of the year 2000+ it could be a compulsory service as part of the national planning for population design and control. Already eugenists point out that infertility ranks as a social problem because people of high intellectual ability are relatively less fertile than other sections of the community, and as a result the Western nations are not reproducing from those whom the State regards as its best men and women, but from inferior stock. Childlessness among the right sort of potential parents can be viewed as a serious problem for a society fashioned and maintained on some kind of national plan.

Aids as regards fertility in marriages which are involuntarily sterile will increase on the medical side with new treatments. Ovaries, or pieces of ovaries, removed from women during gynaecological operations at the Johns Hopkins Hospital in Baltimore have been used for experiments by Dr R. G. Edwards of the Physiological Laboratory at Cambridge University.[1] He dissected out the cells called oöcytes and put them in a tissue culture. Most of the cells can be successfully taken through stages of development until they become matured eggs, ready for fertilisation as they would grow in natural conditions in a woman's body during the mid-phase of the menstrual cycle. The Cambridge experiments resulted in some of the dissected ovaries yielding up to sixty eggs which, of course, is a minute fraction of the potential egg production of a young human female. However, the success in bringing the cells to maturity has given a clue on how to stimulate growth in a woman's own ovaries by hormone treatment.

This procedure would not, however, induce fertility in a woman whose uterine tubes are blocked and are therefore unable to release a mature egg to a position where the male sperm can fertilise it. As a possible way to overcome this problem, Dr Edwards, and Dr R. M. Steptoe of Oldham (Lancs) General Hospital, have succeeded in growing fertilised eggs in the laboratory. The growth was supervised for about five days, at which stage the egg could in theory be placed in the female uterus to develop normally through the nine months of pregnancy. This implant would clearly be an extremely delicate operation, not only because of the minute size of the embryo but on account of the need to select the right time in the potential mother's menstrual cycle to ensure that the fertilised egg was not shed along with the lining of the womb at the end of the monthly period.

A less intricate method of ensuring conception in a woman who is infertile because of some physical inability is to place some of her ova in her uterus by surgical means to coincide with the arrival of her husband's sperm received during intercourse. The anxiety of many childless couples to have a child is so great that the presence of a medical team in a hospital theatre serving as the matrimonial bedroom just prior to intercourse would not be an insuperable objection.

The calculated attitude to sexual intercourse and conception by modern couples anxious to have a child is amply proved by the quietly growing practice of artificial insemination. Since the end of the second world war the number of children born without the parents conceiving through normal intercourse has probably far exceeded a hundred thousand in Europe and the USA, though actual figures are impossible to obtain.

Doctors, of course, do not divulge the identity of their clients without permission, and most parents of artificially inseminated babies understandably do not advertise the fact. What is certain is that throughout the Western world, except perhaps in a few Catholic countries where doctors prefer to conform to the Vatican's rules and recommendations, there are today very many grown men and women, now themselves parents, who were what are popularly but inaccurately known as test-tube babies twenty and thirty years ago.

Artificial insemination might have caused comparatively mild criticism if it had been confined to the AIH process (artificial insemination: husband). In this instance the moral and religious objections have been confined mainly to the question of human interference with natural or divine laws: the fertilisation of a woman when, on account of some physical defect, God or nature apparently desired to prevent it. This can be said to rank beside the Victorian rejection of anaesthesia in childbirth as an evasion of the Biblical edict on bringing forth children in sorrow and the refusal of some Christian sects to permit blood transfusions. A further objection is that AIH entails a form of masturbation to obtain the husband's semen, and an evil means even to a good end is wicked. The folklore about masturbation is almost entirely without any scientific validity and theories about its being sinful are based largely on the Bible story of Onan, which was an incident of incest taboo, and in any event is more relevant to a condemnation of *coitus interruptus* than of masturbation.

AID (artificial insemination: donor) is widely practised in the USA, but in Britain appears to be severely limited and carried out only under conditions of great confidentiality. For psychological and other reasons doctors ready to treat women with AID usually prefer that neither the woman nor her husband should know the identity of the donor, who is selected entirely on his qualities as a human being. He must be healthy, have a good family history, be in the biologically favourable period of twenty-five to forty years of age, and of the same race, build, and intelligence as the woman's husband. Hitherto doctors have preferred that he be a married man and a father, in order to confirm that the donor's fertility is good and no inheritance defects have manifested themselves in his own naturally conceived offspring. Here, apparently, for calculated reasons of eugenics, the basic rule of fidelity in marriage is being deliberately assailed by science.

Disturbing reports have come from the USA of the semen from a type of excellent but standardised American male being used to fertilise twenty and more women. In theory the semen from one donor could be used to fertilise 400 women a week. Even the reports of births to twenty different women and one father provide misgivings about the possibility of eugenically undesirable marriages a couple of decades later. No matter how widely scattered the homes of the donated mothers may be, in a mobile society such as that of the United States the chances of young people in the same age group and of common paternity meeting and marrying are clearly present. Paternity as a profession is emerging as the result of artificial conception techniques. Efficient rationalisation of male sexual services has been achieved in the USA where medical students and hospital housemen can earn a fee of $20 for supplying their semen, which is then stored in phials and deep-frozen at a clinic in Los Angeles. The donors are all of a high IQ, as is to be expected with men who have been successful as medical graduates. On the physical side there are, of course, checks on the medical history and hereditary factors. The phial of semen is classified under a series of headings: blood group, hair and eye colour, race, height, and complexion. These details are provided so that the purchaser can select the characteristics for her baby—either as her personal choice or to match those of her sterile husband. The identity of the donor is kept secret by the clinic in coded records. Up to 2,000 phials of semen are available.

Techniques are apparently not so advanced as in the artificial insemination of animals, as the clinic has frequently to inseminate clients several times at monthly intervals before conception takes place. But in the ideal example of success at the first insemination a woman can purchase conception for $40. By the summer of 1971 eighty-eight babies had been born or were expected as the result of insemination with previously frozen sperm.

While experience in animal husbandry has virtually proved that there is no physical difference in the young conceived through artificial insemination with sperm frozen and stored for a considerable period from animals born after natural copulation, the erosion of human parental responsibilities and the absence of any emotional bond between the parents must be argued as regrettable. The human maternal instinct is more deeply implanted than any other behaviour pattern and a woman whose yearning for a baby is so great that she is prepared to undergo this coldly scientific process is probably capable of overcoming—or suppressing—any feelings of guilt she may have about an unnatural manipulation of her bodily functions. But the eventual effects on the male donor are as unknown as they are evidently ignored. At all stages from near-civilisation onwards the male has had the desire to protect his mate and young and has evinced pride in his offspring. The knowledge that women are being impregnated with his semen and that there are children who are biologically his sons and daughters cannot but have a disturbing effect even on a man of high intelligence.

It seems obvious that in the future, if AID indeed becomes more widely practised—and the incidence of involuntary infertility among married couples who want children makes it inevitable that it will—the State will have to campaign against complete secrecy, or take the easier step of forbidding it by enforcing a record of an AID conception on the birth certificate. This record might at first respect the anonymity of the donor by giving him a serial number in order to provide basic details of paternity when the child applied for a marriage certificate. But with the familiar policy of all modern States to discover everything about every citizen this anonymity would rapidly become just a gesture to the principle of personal privacy. In some national computer bank the donor's identity would be fully documented for the edification of the State's security services, census department, and various government bodies.

Official recognition and social acceptance of AID would enable the present hypocrisies and technical offences to be eradicated. Parents of an AID baby may take the risk of registering the birth as one normally conceived, in which case the husband, in claiming to be the father, is committing perjury. In the present official attitude that such births are illegitimate the deception may also deprive other relatives of their rightful inheritance. By the time these problems of rationalising AID births have been solved as regards the children's legal status and their recognition as offspring of a socially accepted method of conception the current objections of the churches may have been overcome, or more probably, ignored.[2]

The potential influences of AID on family and social life can hardly be calculated at this stage. In the early years the semen had to be used within three or four hours, but advances in freezing techniques made in animal breeding now mean that there are no technical objections to preserving the semen for months and years. The time when a man may father a child long after his death is near, and theories about reproducing unique specimens of humanity, on the grounds of intellectual powers, physical perfection, and so on, are already the day dreams of some biologists.

Whatever form marriage and family patterns take in the future it appears almost inevitable that the State will be forced to attempt to exert control over the number of offspring a union should yield. As an extension of that intervention in the personal lives of men and women it will, as an expected sequence of its policy, proceed to investigate the possibilities of quality control. Today's prophets of war, famine and disease as the consequences of unrestricted population increase may well be the teachers of tomorrow's political and social leaders. They will clash head-on with business managements, for whom every additional baby represents a prospective consumer of the products of industry dependent for its existence and progress by catering for ever-increasing living standards enjoyed by an ever-increasing number of customers. The outcome, even with a degree of compromise, will inevitably be that the State will become the victor. The alternative would be chaos from social pressures as dangerous to trade as to government.

The rationing of babies will present a formidable problem to the twenty-first century's economists and social scientists. Precipitate action to institute a policy of stability of population would quickly result in the average age of the controlled community increasing by up to ten years, with a large proportion over sixty, the desired number under ten, and a violent decrease among the intervening age groups. This situation would make some appeal to the State because an elderly society would be hostile to change, and the established order would be very difficult for the very young—the only other large group—to change, but the nation would be composed of far too many dependants, an enormous burden on the restricted proportion of people of employable age.

On the personal level discreet control of family size would probably be accepted without much objection after the initial disquiet. Propaganda has long since been launched to suggest that the very large family is anti-social. In many Western societies the mother of six and more children is pitied or criticised, not congratulated—unless she is wealthy or a social leader. This distinction on grounds of possessions or birth will not survive a general antipathy to privilege by heritage or money.

The most powerful weapon in the hands of future population controllers will be reliable and aesthetically acceptable contraception. Tens of thousands of babies are born every year only because existing methods of birth control are unreliable, messy, awkward, or potentially dangerous. When the Pill has been modified to have no side-effects and need be taken at less frequent intervals, when such easy methods of contraception as 'morning after' drugs and once-a-year injections for either the men or the woman have been perfected, the number of unwanted babies can be expected greatly to decrease. There are estimates in both Britain and the USA that the number of unwanted babies born each year is about 20 per cent of the total births, even with the benefits of fairly reliable methods of birth control.

Among older British women, those married between 1920 and 1934, who had unwanted children, even though they had hoped to plan their families, the proportion was nearly a quarter. Those married between 1930 and 1934 had an average of 3·2 children in their fertile years; they had desired an average of 1·24.[3] These women spent their early married lives during a period of unemployment, housing shortage, and uncertainty due to the imminence of war. Their daughters have been more ready to have two children or more, but the restriction to a number far below that of which they are capable of bearing, and which in previous generations was usual, indicates how easily women can be persuaded to limit their families to a low figure.

Nor does it seem likely that the State would have much trouble in persuading wives who had infringed the national advice—carefully separated from direct legislation in the democracies—to have their pregnancies terminated. Abortion, the ancient method of family limitation along with infanticide, has already become respectable: a service provided free of charge by the State. When induced abortion was still a criminal act in Britain (except for a very limited number of cases) the Royal Commission on Population estimated that 11·4 of pregnancies did not go their full time. In pre-war Berlin abortions were estimated to exceed the number of births, and in the USA, prior to legislation permitting abortion in some states, one estimate was of 700,000 illegal abortions a year. In England and Wales, when termination of pregnancy was legalised subject to medical approval, the number of abortions rose from 54,819 in 1969 to 128,774 in 1971. No civilised country will depend on abortions to control the birth rate on this scale for very long, not merely on moral grounds, but because abortion is clearly the most expensive and dangerous method of birth control. The practical and sensible policy will be to provide free, reliable, and harmless contraceptives as a State service, and irrespective of sex, age, or status of the applicants.

While State-specified limitation on the number of children would therefore seem to be reasonably assured of acquiescent acceptance by the newlyweds of tomorrow, in that it would set a maximum average of a little over two children—rather higher than the average wife evidently wants—there could be a source of unrest if for some reason the State demanded that a couple must regard it as a civic duty to have the authorised number of babies according to some eugenic or social regulation despite their wish to have one child or none at all. However useful it might be for the State to concern itself with breeding the kind of human beings it preferred, reaction of the individual would be violent. Such overall and precise planning of the population would therefore seem to be a procedure set well in the future.

The simplest way to change the conception of human life, from the present haphazard mating of two people who happen to have been attracted to one another to a calculated and approved production of progeny, will be to maintain personal medical histories of every citizen in far greater detail than at present. The comparative anonymity of the personal records kept by the State today, with overall totals of cases of disease, injury, causes of death, and so on, omitting identification of the individuals concerned, will be changed with computer banks containing complete medical histories of the 'womb to tomb' type on the forebears of every citizen. These records will provide data on the suitability of a couple for breeding. Checks on this information would be carried out when the application for a marriage licence was made. In some instances the application would inevitably be rejected. This need not cause undue alarm. For generations society has obeyed or at least considered taboos on marriage between persons closely related, of different race or colour, even of differences in age, social status, and wealth.

Population control would have to be based on substituting quality for quantity. The pressures of a technological society, with its insatiable hunger for brain power, will make encouragement of selective breeding on a voluntary basis attractive. The benefits might be slow, but the descendants of two or three generations of parents, all with a high IQ, would themselves have an IQ of a higher figure. Although breeding humans to exploit hereditary qualities would be a long process and fraught with risks of deterioration in more qualities than the one or two it improved, there would be a better case for eradicating hereditary defects.

About one baby in every hundred born in Britain suffers from some genetic defect, but survives, either because it can live with the defect or is kept alive by scientific aid; it is estimated that 15 million people in the USA are living with defects serious enough to affect their daily lives. Most aberrations originate before birth, and more than a thousand genetic defects, ranging from comparatively unimportant ones like colour-blindness, to disastrous examples such as those of monstrosity and imbecility, have been identified. Nature destroys many of these abnormal embryos by spontaneous abortion, stillbirth, or an independent existence ended in a few hours, but a child born alive will be successfully helped to

L

survive more and more frequently as medical skill increases. The efficiency of modern death control is the cause of over-population to a greater extent than the inefficiency of birth control, and techniques to postpone death seem to advance faster than those to prevent birth. In the case of babies who would die if not given costly and continuous treatment, a balance will have to be struck between the compassion for the individual suffering through no fault of his own and a regard for the general good of the community. Many doctors and nurses can recount incidents where a monstrous baby has quickly died because nothing was done to sustain its life. Such a harrowing decision is best left to the individual doctor. Professional or official rulings about it could be nothing but a preliminary to enforced euthanasia and State-run gas chambers.

History is crammed with the names of men and women who have inspired and benefited humanity, but who would never have been born if a bigoted insistence on the rules of eugenics had existed when they proved to be the sort of 'freaks' mankind badly needs. But the computer-based technocracy of tomorrow is unlikely to be interested in gambling on the occasional birth of an artist, poet or philosopher, or even a clown, when science offers the certainty of viable and near-standardised human beings, equipped with approved IQ, stature, expectation of life, and all the other required attributes of the Brave New Man.

That situation may well be beyond the immediate horizon of the biologists' and politicians' thoughts. But far closer is the ambition to change the climate of public opinion so that a sexual act intended to cause the conception of human life is no longer the private and personal concern of a man and woman, but an activity in which the State insists on taking an interest, at first approving or disapproving, and in time authorising or forbidding. Yet such a forecast of official intrusion will be a distasteful aggravation rather than a destroyer of family life. It will be merely a new topic of dispute, and the individual will resist in order to obtain a compromise. Ever since the series of modern revolutionary developments in the means of production, and the consequent growth of urbanised communities of many millions of people, enormous pressures have been exerted on family life to enforce changes. They have come from both sides of the community, the rulers and ruled. The 'common man', literate, educated, and emancipated, has insisted on enjoying more and more of the privileges previously restricted to a minority. The semblance of freedom of thought and action which this change has provided has encouraged a desire for independence in personal living. Marriage has become a sexual adventure in which the emotional impulses of two persons are regarded as the reason for what used to be called its solemnisation, but is now chiefly an official registration for social and economic reasons.

The State, even when it attempts direct organisation of its citizens' lives, has hitherto had to acquiesce in this haphazard creation of new families as a method of minimising social and political discontent. A Freudian-engrossed society has been brainwashed into believing that sex makes the world go round. Traditions of family law lapse. Ancestors are consigned to oblivion. The descendants demand to be independent of ties. Tolerance has replaced self-restraint.

While the modern State finds it convenient to condone a steady extension of personal freedom in sexual and social activities as a form of safety valve, with all the disturbance of the *status quo* which must result, it has to intervene when this haphazard and quixotic method of creating a family yields offspring, supporting and fashioning the existence of a two-generation family for its brief life while doing little to maintain the structure of the group through its older members and relatives by marriage or blood.

'Family planning' would have been thought by earlier generations to be a worthy scheme to construct a family of grandparents, parents, children, and relatives in a stable and strong entity well equipped to look after itself. Today the term refers only to the mechanics of conception and how to avoid this consequence of sexual pleasure if children are not desired. The State deems itself the best authority on the size of this modern nuclear family, and having set itself up as master, judge, and adviser, it insists on shouldering or supervising many of the duties of parenthood. Vast sums of money, skill and labour are expended on rearing a new generation in the manner which the State, and not necessarily the parents, consider desirable. A smaller but still formidable amount of ingenuity and energy is available for the purpose of transferring the burden of caring for the family's aged, sick, and insane so that the nuclear family shall not be incommoded by the weaker members.

This stream of official activity is, admittedly, a mark of an enlightened civilisation where the individual, and particularly tomorrow's individual, is regarded as important. But the attitude has resulted in the attempted demotion of the family as the foremost social unit and weakened the loyalties of kinship without producing substitutes satisfying to the human heart and mind.

The State is by definition hostile to any group within its body which puts its own loyalties first and could become large enough to present a rebellious front. Repression of powerful groups of kinsfolk is aided by the conditions of modern urban civilisation, which the State appears at least tacitly to foster. Cities are allowed to expand to an unwieldy size in which pride in birthplace or dwelling place is difficult. Mobility of employment and easy transport facilities have destroyed the old settled communities in which everybody knew everybody else and many were related. Barrack-type blocks of apartments provide a battery-hen existence in which scores of families are hardly aware of the names of their neighbours on the next floor. Bigger schools and colleges, sited for official convenience instead of a regard for community life, brings hundreds and sometimes thousands of children and juveniles temporarily together in an anonymous mass. Television is a mass entertainment enjoyed in isolation. The workplace is rarely part of the family home, and frequently miles away from the dwelling area. Men spend most of their working days travelling to and from their workplace and in the company of thousands of comparative strangers spread over acres of factory space. Women either imitate their husbands and work among other women whom they hardly know or languish in frustrating boredom in a characterless living unit. The friendly shop on the corner has been replaced by the self-service supermarket, and the pub of character by a chain inn, complete with car park for the nomads who are its mainstay. The sports arena is filled with thousands of strangers, many regarded as enemies. The comforting companionship of the weekly church meeting is unknown to millions.

The State prides itself that this pattern of living is progressive and popular. It cushions its citizens against all worldly troubles with welfare services, good wages, monetary benefits, and palliatives in the shape of alcohol, nicotine, entertainment, and gambling. At every election the electorate is wooed with offers of still more of these official contributions to the happiness and suffocating comfort of the miniature family's life.

That twentieth-century urban man and woman are finding that this State-planned existence is unsatisfactory can be seen in the prevalence of social unrest, apparently the more violent the more affluent and cossetted the nation concerned. Demoralised by lack of identifiable loyalties, each generation is ignoring its own family kin and seeking cohesion by age. Minority groups find reason for loyalty within themselves by displaying hostility to the majority. Demonstrators coalesce and hardly care what they demonstrate about so long as they march together to protest and defy 'them'.

Nationalism of a type born from the ruins of the unwieldy political alliances and empires after two world wars, is being fragmented still further and then re-formed as people turn to a grouping small enough for the human mind to accept as representing a group of individuals and not a shape on a world map. The states of the USA battle tenaciously against the encroachment of federal rule. The Basques, the Jews, the Scots, the Welsh, the Bretons, and scores of other groups with little more than a folk memory of past individuality and independence fight and campaign in order to opt out of the mass societies, irrespective of the practical considerations of economics and security. The European Common Market, designed by bureaucracy to enhance the wealth and security of its member States and their citizens, is regarded with suspicion by many of those it is designed to benefit; almost forgotten and recently despised feelings of patriotism are revived as a protest against the soulless, materialistic concept of a European conglomerate.

These attempts to retrieve the satisfaction and one-ness of the kinship group can in the long run only be suppressed by force, and few modern States dare risk force as a permanent policy. Within the new kinship groups the family units are discovering renewed strength, for in most of these independence movements unquestioned loyalty of the families of the adherents is vital. It is evident that all members are prepared to sacrifice materialistic benefits for the deeply ingrained sense of belonging, which gives a meaning to life in the mind of the social animal called man.

Both sides—and the State and the citizen are steadily moving to different sides—will have to seek a compromise in tomorrow's world if the twin desires for individual freedom of living and the maintenance of social order are to be met. If society is to continue on its present technological path—and there can be no turning back—both marriage and the family are due to pass through a long period of transition.

Some of the changes envisaged, and now being prepared, by the technocrats who are moving into the political scene, are Orwellian nightmares. Others, if one can get rid of prejudice and nostalgia for the not-so-good old days, are a happy dream of a future in which the injustices that have marked the imperfect culture of social life in the past may be eradicated.

The developments and changes which have been foreshadowed in the possible trends of family life in the future are no reason to suggest that the present day marks the last chapter in the history of ordered and socially desirable units for the comfort and contentment of one generation and the creation of the succeeding one. As has so often been said, marriage is designed for man and not man for marriage. Every society creates for itself a pattern of communal living which it believes is the best for its survival, and experience has always taught the lesson that nihilism is unworkable, both for the well-being of the individual and the stability of the community to which he belongs.

The human family may have come into existence to satisfy biological needs, but it was uplifted when it was given rules in order to protect the weak, encourage the strong, and enable a group of both sexes and all ages to live in security and harmony. The original motive was a natural volition engendered by sexual attraction and the instinct to beget young; the subsequent development an artificial plan imposed to control and assist the former. The result has invariably been an almost incredibly successful compromise between selfish fulfilment and unselfish constraint.

The technocracies of the future will at their peril attempt to regiment the lives of their subjects without regard for human need for personal satisfaction in their relationships. The prophets of social science appear to be talking about the State benignly approving a sexual revolution having all the trappings of freedom amounting to licence, which will conceal a cold and calculated dictatorship of every man-woman relationship which develops towards the natural production of offspring. If these trends are correctly identified the arbiters of social existence will be ignoring the fact that the family is the primary social institution and any formal recognition of the partnership called marriage a subsidiary to it. The family can exist without marriage but marriage is pointless without the family in the broadest sense of the term. Any endeavour to destroy the family by grouping people in some politically formulated mass will end in failure, and possibly catastrophic upheaval.

The formal institution of marriage as we have known it for most of the Christian era in the West may soon be changing and extending to forms that can hardly be imagined, let alone approved. But the family, with its ancestors, its contemporary members, and its successors, will find stability and recognition as it has since *homo sapiens* first took a mate and stayed beside her to rear their offspring.

Notes and Bibliography for this chapter are on page 178

Notes and Bibliographies

NOTES

1 *Sex, Marriage and Family in a Changing Society* (pp 7-28)

1 Figures from a survey by Armand Georges quoted by John and Janet Newell in *Bachelor Living* (1968).
2 Quoted in 'Group Counselling' issued to teachers and youth leaders.
3 Figures from the Registrar General in the Annual Abstract of Statistics (HMSO)
4 Estimates by René Dubos and Maya Pines for the *Life* Science Library.
5 Records of the Divorce Registry.
6 In 1870-2 the percentage of illegitimate births was 6. This figure was not exceeded until 1943 (6.5). The wartime peak was 9.1 in 1945.
7 Figures in 'Social Trends', issued by the Central Statistical Office in 1970.
8 In 1971 the Greater London Council approved in principle the granting of mortgages to unmarried couples and, financial qualifications acceptable, to unmarried mothers.
9 Figures from the Weiner Library Report no 4, 1970-1, by Ya'akov Hurwitz.

BIBLIOGRAPHY

Anshen, R. N. *The Family: Its Functions and Destiny* (1949). A serious study of modern social cultures.
Buber, M. *Path in Utopia* (1949). Vivid account of life in a kibbutz.
Church of England. *Putting Asunder* (1966). A report on the Church's attitude to divorce by a committee set up by the Archbishop of Canterbury under the chairmanship of the Bishop of Exeter.
Fletcher, Ronald. *Britain in the Sixties: The Family and Marriage* (1962).

M

An analysis of contemporary family life which provides an encouraging report on its present health and an optimistic forecast for the future.

Friedan, Betty. *The Feminine Mystique* (1963). This book inspired the women's liberation movements in the USA and Europe. The author is the founder of the most influential of the movements, NOW (National Organisation of Women).

Goldberg, Sidney (editor). *This is Israel* (1970). An excellent account of the modern kibbutz is included in this survey.

Graveson, R. H., Crane, F. R. (editors). *A Century of Family Law, 1857-1957* (1957). History of the changes occurring since the first divorce legislation, changes in illegitimacy laws, etc.

Houriet, Robert. *Getting Back Together* (New York 1971). Published as this chapter was being written, it is the best account so far available on the modern communes and group marriages in the USA.

Mead, Margaret. *Male and Female* (1949). This lavishly documented book, by an international authority, gives her answer to the problems of men's and women's sexuality in the twentieth century.

Millett, Kate. *Sexual Politics* (1970). A work which is regarded as the 'Bible' of the women's liberation movement, and is an objective survey of the alleged evils of sex inequality.

Pospishil, Mgr Victor. *Divorce and Remarriage* (New York 1967). A critical survey of Roman Catholic marriage laws providing the arguments for and against changes which have subsequently aroused controversy in the USA.

Segre, V. D. *Israel, a Society in Transition* (Oxford 1970). An authoritative work on the social influences of the kibbutz on the emerging nation of Israel.

2 Birth of the Human Family (pp 29-50)

NOTES

1 This period of widespread glacial activity was comparatively mild compared with preceding ice ages. The Great Ice Age, the last of at least four periods to cause widespread glaciation, is estimated to have begun 1¾ million years ago. The dates of the Late Glacial Phase given here are necessarily vague and the subject of continuing controversy, partly because of the variation of climatic changes in areas where man existed.

2 The fossil remains of Peking man, excavated between 1927 and 1937, included fourteen skulls and 150 teeth. They were lost when in transit after hostilities between China and Japan broke out, but casts had been made and taken to the American Museum of Natural History in New York.

3 In the United Kingdom over the past century the ratio of live births of males has varied from 1,037 to 1,065 per 1,000 female births. Deaths of infants under one year of age modify the difference, male mortality always being the greater. This ratio is apparently a permanent one unless the future brings scientific interference.

4 The best known of these figurines, the so-called Venus of Willendorf found in the Danube valley of Lower Austria in 1908, is of late palaeolithic culture: circa 28,000-18,000 BC.

5 A culture dating from 28,000-18,000 BC named after La Gravette, a
   rock shelter in the Dordogne region of France.
6 The houses of Skara Brae which can be seen today are the most recent
   of at least three communities built on the site.

BIBLIOGRAPHY

Bibby, Geoffrey. *The Testimony of the Spade* (1956). The story of early
    man in Europe, principally in connection with Scandinavian and
    Central Europe excavations.
Childe, V. Gordon. *What Happened in History* (1942). A general story of
    early man's development by one of the foremost prehistorians, and
    director of many digs in Britain, notably Skara Brae. Professor Childe's
    The Dawn of European Civilisation (1925, revised 1950) is a standard
    work on agricultural colonisation and its economic and social effects.
Coon, Carleton S. *The History of Man* (New York, 1954). A vivid and
    lavishly illustrated book on the social life of prehistoric man. The
    narrative continues to modern times.
Hill, J. B. and Hill, Helen D. *Genetics and Human Heredity* (1955). A
    detailed study of the effects of heredity on the development of the
    individual.
McFarland, David and Jill. *An Introduction to the Study of Behaviour*
    (Oxford, 1969). This work is in two parts—animal behaviour and
    human behaviour. It is not a science text, but deals with the biological
    and philosophical factors involved in behaviour patterns.
Morris, Desmond. *The Naked Ape* (1967). The well-known study of
    man's sexual and social habits. The author combines his own observa-
    tions as a zoologist with the findings of palaeontology and the in-
    formation derived from the study of behaviour among monkeys and
    apes.
Piggott, Stuart (editor). *The Dawn of Civilisation* (1962). This co-operative
    venture, with the text by fourteen leading archaeologists, rightly claims
    to be the first world survey of the early cultures of mankind, and
    covers half a million years of prehistory. It is lavishly illustrated with
    reconstructions and photographs, a large proportion in colour.
Solecki, Ralph S. *Shanidar : the First Flower People* (New York, 1971).
    An important new work by the leader of an expedition excavating a
    Neanderthal site in Iraq. Dr Solecki's evidence helps to disprove the
    earlier theories that Neanderthal man was a brutish, amoral creature.
Southwick, C. H. (editor). *Primate Social Behaviour* (Princeton, 1963).
    Papers on modern research for the expert zoologist, but full of
    fascinating information for the informed layman.
Tinbergen, N. *The Study of Instinct* (Oxford, 1951). A scientific work
    explaining the processes of instinct as compared with patterns of
    behaviour.
Wendt, Herbert. *I Looked for Adam* (1957). This German writer describes
    the work of archaeologists, biologists, and geneticists who have pieced
    together the history of early man.
Westermarck, Edward. *The History of Human Marriage* (5th edition,
    3 vols, 1921). This standard work is listed here, as it begins with a
    long account of the origin of marriage. It is the most comprehensive
    survey available, inevitably referred to by all subsequent writers on

marriage, the family, and social cultures. Professor Westermarck's volumes cover all peoples everywhere at all stages of man's history. The authorities quoted by the author cover virtually every reliable writer whose material was available at the time of the original writing and subsequent revisions.

Winchester, A. M. *Heredity* (1964). An outline of the principles of genetics for the general reader.

Zuckerman, S. *The Social Life of Monkeys and Apes* (1932). Probably the most authoritative description of the behaviour patterns of these animals.

3   Family Experiments in Early Civilisations (pp 51-69)

NOTE

1   Genesis 2, 24.

BIBLIOGRAPHY

Baumgartel, E. J. *The Cultures of Prehistoric Egypt* (Oxford, 1955). A valuable account of the early social and religious practices of the Egyptians.

Bertholet, Alfred (translated by A. K. Dallas). *A History of Hebrew Civilisation* (1926). An excellent accompaniment to the Old Testament for a study of ancient Israel's culture.

Bloch, Raymond. *The Origins of Rome* (English edition, 1960). A vivid reconstruction of life in Rome up to the birth of the Republic, and particularly valuable for its description of the migrations, culture, laws and religion of the Roman people.

Breasted, J. H. *A History of Egypt* (1911). An early, but still standard, work for the general reader.

Burn, Andrew R. *The World of Hesiod* (1936). An excellent description of life in Greece in the ninth century BC.

Chrimes, K. M. T. *Ancient Sparta* (Manchester, 1949). Particularly informative on the disciplinary policies which moulded the life of every man, woman and child in Sparta.

Freeman, K. *The Work and Life of Solon* (1926). A comprehensive survey of conditions in Greece when Solon reorganised the constitution, thereby creating a class system and a new concept of law and morality —the effects of which are to be seen in our democracy today.

Gardiner, Sir Alan. *Egypt of the Pharaohs* (Oxford, 1961). This well-known authority on ancient Egypt covers his subject from its primitive origins to Alexander the Great.

Gibbon, Edward. *The Decline and Fall of the Roman Empire* (edited by H. R. Trevor-Roper) (1966). The eighteenth-century work of Gibbon is, of course, one of the foremost examples of historical literature ever written. The version cited here is a masterly abridgement for the modern reader, either as an introduction to the wealth of information in the original six volumes or as an insight, complete in itself, into Gibbon's unsurpassed knowledge of classical Rome.

Havell, H. L. *Republican Rome: Her Conquests, Manners and Institutions* (1913). From the vast number of sources available on Roman history, this work proved particularly valuable to the author as regards social and family life.

Kramer, S. N. *From the Tablets of Sumer* (1954). A comprehensive survey of the Babylonian culture, with information on the code of Hammurabi, including laws relating to marriage and the family.

Michell, H. *Sparta* (Cambridge, 1964). A scholarly but lively account of this unique city state.

Rostovtzeff, M. *A History of the Ancient World*, Vol 1 (Oxford, 1925). A compact and factual review of the Athenian states.

Sinclair, T. A. (translator). *Works and Days* (by Hesiod). This poem is a remarkable portrait of the agricultural classes in the heroic period of Greece and includes Hesiod's views on marriage and women.

4   The Christian Compromise (pp 70-80)

NOTES

1   The modern and conventional spelling of a name known to the Romans as Boudicca. The original Celtic form is unknown.
2   Corinthians, 7, 1.
3   Corinthians, 7, 9.
4   See *The Theology of Tertullian*. R. E. Roberts (1924).

BIBLIOGRAPHY

Barrow, G. W. S. *Feudal Britain* (1956). Invaluable as a study of the rigid division of the classes and its influence on personal life under feudalism.

Cambridge Medieval History (1929). This work provides the standard material on the period. Notable in regard to family life and culture is 'The Triumph of Christianity', T. M. Lindsay, in vol 1.

Chadwick, N. *Celtic Britain* (1963). A concise account of the people who invaded Britain after circa 800 BC and created powerful tribal communities.

Clark, J. G. D. *Prehistoric Europe—the Economic Basis* (1952). The author shows how manufacture and agriculture contributed to the social development of our remote ancestors.

Haskins, C. H. *Normans in European History* (1916). Valuable for an understanding of the basically Scandinavian attitude to family life which pervaded most of Europe after the Viking and Norman conquests and colonisation.

Haverfield, F. J. *The Romanisation of Roman Britain* and *Roman Occupation of Britain* (Oxford, 1924). These two well-known works provide a complete survey of the degree to which customs of Rome were implanted in Britain.

Hodgkin, R. H. *A History of the Anglo-Saxons* (1935). Deals with the customs and policies of the tribes migrating westwards to Britain, whose culture was later absorbed and adapted by the Christian concept of marriage and family.

Holmes, George. *The Later Middle Ages (1272-1485)* (1962). A general account of medieval England and Western Europe up to the Renaissance and the beginning of the Tudor period.

Lecky, W. E. H. *History of European Morals* (1881). This work covers the moral concepts in countries influenced by Rome from the reign of Augustus to the death of Charlemagne. The subject is treated with the impartiality for which this Victorian historian and philosopher was notable.

Slesser, Sir Henry. *The Middle Ages in the West* (1950). Excellent history of the social changes spreading through Europe.

Stenton, D. M. *English Society in the Early Middle Ages* (1951). A very thorough and sensitive study of day-to-day existence under feudalism.

5 *The Changing Role of the Family* (pp 81-99)

NOTES

1 During the sixteenth century some 10,000 parishes in England and Wales had endeavoured to organise welfare services to replace those of the monasteries. Many appointed overseers to collect and distribute money. Some ran houses of correction and workhouses. These activities applied only to church parishes, leaving many communities untouched. The Elizabethan Poor Laws rationalised these varied welfare projects.

2 The Malthus essay was originally published anonymously in 1798. Its 1801 revival was encouraged by the first population census in Britain made in that year. The total was just under 11 millions. Previous estimates of some reliability include the totals inferred from the Domesday survey (1086) of a population in England and Wales of about 1 million, and the calculation of Gregory King (1695) with a total of 5½ millions.

3 A personal account of the trial is included in Mrs Besant's autobiography *Through Storm to Peace*.

BIBLIOGRAPHY

Calhoun, A. W. *Social History of the American Family* (New York, 1917). This work includes interesting material from private letters and public records during the Colonial phase of North America.

Cole, G. D. H. and Postgate, Raymond. *The Common People* (1930). A detailed survey on the social effects of the Industrial Revolution on the people of town and country.

Fay, C. R. *Life and Labour in the Nineteenth Century* (Cambridge, 1920). A well-documented account of customs and economic conditions after the Napoleonic Wars.

Flinn, Michael W. *An Economic and Social History of Britain* (1961). Written mainly for students, this work provides a broad survey, with detailed treatment by topics in each of the three parts, among which those on urban and rural life, population growth, social legislation, and social movements are relevant to family life.

Folsom, Joseph Kirk. *The Family and Democratic Society* (1949). This historical record, by an American professor of sociology, includes a section on the pioneer families settling in New England and the other colonies, with excerpts from contemporary material.

Goodsell, Willystine. *A History of the Family as a Social and Educational Institution* (New York, 1917). While this work is a general history of the family, it is mentioned here for its vivid and detailed material on early English colonists in America.

Hammond, J. L. and Barbara. *The Bleak Age* (1934). The well-known study of the lives of working people in the first half of the nineteenth century is particularly valuable for its material on the 'new' Poor Law, education, and public welfare services.

Howard, George. *Guardians of the Queen's Peace* (1953). This book on law and order enforcement in Britain includes much material on social and moral legislation during and after the Reformation, and under the Commonwealth.

Newton, A. P. *The Colonising Activities of the English Puritans* (New York, 1914). A carefully documented account of social and family life in seventeenth-century America.

Trevor-Roper, H. R. *Religion, the Reformation, and Social Change* (1967) and *The Rise of Christian Europe* (1965). Essential reading for the serious student, and including original sources.

6 *Men and Women in Social Revolt* (pp 100-13)

NOTES

1 The word Suffragette was unknown until 1906, when a journalist on Northcliffe's *Daily Mail* coined it.

2 Written by Queen Victoria to Theodore Martin, biographer of the Prince Consort. The comment remained unpublished during the queen's life.

3 In *The Subjection of Women*, published in 1866, and written by Mill in 1858 as a memorial to his wife.

4 Trial marriage as the description of a legal but temporary union was first suggested by an American writer, Elsie Clews Parsons, in *The Family*, published in 1912. Her theory was that it would curb prostitution. The view aroused a storm of criticism and was soon forgotten.

5 Proposed by Dr Knight in a medical paper in 1924 and reproduced in the *U.S. Journal of Social Hygiene*.

6 A degree of simplification of divorce proceedings authorised by legislation in 1965 and 1968 has moderately increased the number of dissolved marriages in the Soviet Union—about 600,000 a year in the 1970s.

BIBLIOGRAPHY

Engels, Frederick. *The Origin of the Family, Private Property, and the State* (1884, translated by Ernest Unterman, 1902). The account, ranging from descriptions of prehistoric, Athenian and Roman family life to that of nineteenth-century Red Indians and Germans, is inevitably politically slanted to the author's views. In its time cheap editions sold in large numbers, particularly in the USA, and the book is therefore valuable as a picture of radical thinking about family life at the close of the nineteenth century under Marxist influence.

Fulford, Roger. *Votes for Women* (1957). A delightful record with rich material on the lives of the women who campaigned for such women's rights as suffrage, marital independence, birth control, 'free love', etc.

Goodsell, Willystine. *A History of the Family as a Social and Educational Institution* (New York, 1917). This study covers the development of the family and marriage from primitive times, but is of most value for its survey of the situation in the nineteenth century and the reforms immediately prior to the first world war. American conditions are naturally given prominence, but they are compared with those in Britain.

Metcalfe, A. E. *Woman's Effort—a Chronicle of Fifty Years' Struggle for Citizenship* (1917). Although this book deals chiefly with the campaign for women's suffrage it also contains a mass of information on the status of women as wives and mothers. Asquith paid it the wry compliment of calling it 'a curious book'.

Reuter, Edward Byron, and Runner, Jessie Ridgway. *The Family* (New York, 1931). This long work by American sociologists contains extracts from books, or essays, by the best-known authorities on marriage, sex, and family of the period. It is among the best sources of information on the culture and thinking of the American family before the second world war.

Utechin, S. V. *Everyman's Concise Encyclopaedia of Russia* (1961). More than 2,000 articles on every aspect of Russian life provide in condensed form information for the general reader.

Webb, Sidney and Beatrice. *Soviet Communism: a New Civilisation* (1936). A somewhat rose-tinted picture of the USSR, but an authoritative and first-hand description of Russian family life up to the Stalin era.

7 Oriental Concept of Sex and Family Life (pp 114-27)

BIBLIOGRAPHY

Aston, W. G. *Shinto, the Way of the Gods* (1905). One of the first—and best—studies by a Western writer of this Japanese religion.

Benedict, R. *The Chrysanthemum and the Sword* (Boston, 1946). An American's affectionate but erudite study of Japanese culture.

Creel, Herlee Glessner. *The Birth of China* (1936). The history of a nation which has retained most of its family traditions through interminable political changes.

Legge, James. *The Life and Teachings of Confucius* (1902). A valuable treatise on a world-wide religion and its founder.

Levy, R. *An Introduction to the Sociology of Islam* (1933). A long and detailed work on the social influences of the religion of Mohammed.

Maraini, Fosco (translated by Eric Mosbacher). *Meeting with Japan* (1959). A beautifully produced guide book which treats its subject 'in depth', giving the background to the present culture of the Japanese nation.

Martindale, Don. *Social Life and Cultural Change* (Princeton, NJ, 1962). Long sections of this book are concerned with Chinese and Indian social customs from primitive times to the present day.

Oldenberg, Hermann (translated by W. Hoey). *Buddha: his Life, his Doctrines* (1928). Useful for understanding the attitude to marriage and family of about one-third of the world's peoples.

Venkateswara, S. V. *Indian Culture through the Ages* (1928). Deals with

Indian literature and art, but also includes considerable material on marriage and family customs.

Wheeler, Sir Mortimer. *The Cambridge History of India* (Cambridge, 1953. A rich source of the religious and social cultures of the subcontinent.

8   Experimental Family Structures Today (pp 128-50)

NOTES

1   In 1968-9 50,200 women were full-time students at British universities. The number increases by 3-5,000 a year.

2   Percentages of 1968 divorces by duration of marriage were: up to 4 years: 13·6, 5-9 years: 31·8, 10-14 years: 21·4, 15-19 years: 13·5, 20 years and over: 19·7.

3   British courts appear to regard bigamy as a serious crime only if there is evidence of callous deception, or, in earlier times, of a fraudulent ceremony in order to obtain control of the wealth of the duped woman. Otherwise, sentences can be nominal, as in the mid-nineteenth century when a judge sentenced a pauper to one day's imprisonment, advising him that he was wicked not to have found £2,000 to pay for the cost of a Bill to legalise the termination of his first marriage.

4   The example of the Metropolitan Community Church has been followed by the American Orthodox Church in New York with solemnisation of 'holy union' between homosexuals. In San Francisco the Glide Memorial Methodist Church blesses 'pledges of commitment' by homosexual couples.

5   Estimates of reported sex changes since the end of the second world war by hormone therapy or surgery are more than 1,000 in all countries, excluding the communist bloc. While external sex features are changed the internal organs of sex remain the same: treated transsexuals cannot become a parent in their new sexual category.

BIBLIOGRAPHY

Himes, Norman. *Medical History of Contraception* (1936). An interesting survey of the varied methods adopted in an endeavour to control birth from classical times to the pre-Pill era.

Johnson, Stanley. *Life without Birth* (1970). This book, based on a study of world population on behalf of the United Nations Association of the USA, describes the population explosion and outlines possible schemes in the future for both voluntary and State control of the size of families.

Lofthouse, W. F. *The Family and the State* (1944). An expansion of a lecture given at the Methodists' Conference in 1944, reflecting the Christian attitude to the situation of the family vis-a-vis a co-operative or hostile State.

Mead, Margaret. *Coming of Age in Samoa* (1928) and *Growing up in New Guinea* (1930). These classics, referred to by virtually every modern writer on marriage, sex, and family, are cited here because their relevance, aside from the fascinating material on allegedly primitive and simple communities, is on the fundamentals of family life which are now in a state of flux in advanced societies.

Russell, Bertrand. *Marriage and Morals* (1932). Essential reading for an appreciation of modern philosophical attitudes to man-woman relationships.

Seward, Georgene H. *Sex and the Social Order* (1946). A study of the effects of sex difference on the lives of ordinary people.

Westermarck, Edward. *The Future of Marriage in Western Civilisation* (1936). In this work, published when the author was seventy-four, he summarises his views based on the years of research he spent in writing his classic work *History of Human Marriage* (see Bibliography for Chapter Two).

Zimmerman, C. C. *Family and Civilisation* (1947). An interesting view of the contribution of family life to the materialistic and spiritual advances of mankind.

9 *Science as the Family's Dictator* (pp 151-68)

NOTES

1 Reported in *Nature*, 8 January, 1971.

2 It seems unlikely that any major change by Church or State as regards the policy on AID can be expected for some time. The commission set up by the Archbishop of Canterbury in 1948 condemned the technique without any qualifications. A Home Office report in 1960 opposed AID because of the problems of inheritance it would create.

3 Figures from the Papers of the Royal Commission on Population (vol 1) (1949).

BIBLIOGRAPHY

Huxley, Julian; Haddon, A. C.; Carr-Saunders, A. M. *We Europeans* (1935). A famous work on the genetic differences between human groups, and though written nearly forty years ago, an up-to-date description of the task of mankind to recognise the place of biological factors in the social order.

Leach, Gerald. *The Biocrats* (1970). Essential reading for appreciation of the modern developments in science's techniques for human breeding.

Toffler, Alvin. *Future Shock* (1970). This work by a controversial American sociologist is a thoughtful if disturbing survey of the probable, and perhaps inevitable, trends of marriage, family, and child-bearing in the twenty-first century.

Index

social culture of, 55-7

Japan; family life in, 116; religion of, 117-8; wife's status in, 117; divorce in, 118

Jews (*see* Israel)

Justinian, Emperor; divorce law of, 16

Kelleher, Mgr; views on Catholic divorce and re-marriage, 18

Khirokta (Cyprus), 43

Kibbutzim (Israeli communes), 26-7

Kinsey report, 142

Knight, Dr M. M.; idea for childless marriage, 109

Knowlton, Dr Charles; writes contraception manual, 98

Kolkhoz (Russian farming commune), 110

Kollontay, Aleksandra (advocate of 'free love'); 111

Lesbianism; in Athens, 61; modern attitude to, 146

Life; expectation of, 14

Lower Paleolithic man, 39

Malthus, Thomas, 97

Mao-tse Tung, 121

Marriage bureaux, 12

Marriage statistics, 13

Married Women's Property Acts, 101

Marx, Karl, 104, 112

Maryland; feudalistic colonisation of, 87

Matrimonium justum (Roman form of marriage), 66

Mesolithic man, 40

Mill, John Stuart, 104

Milton, John; on divorce, 85

Minors; marriage of, 10

Mohammed, 115; *see also* Islam

Mormons, 134-5

Moshav (Israeli commune), 26

Napoleonic wars; social effects of, 90

National Marriage Guidance Council, 11

Nazi breeding experiments, 59, 151

Neolithic man, 43

Nightingale, Florence; views on family life, 103

Normans; social culture of, 79

Old age; social problems of, 138; statistics, 139; sexuality in, 140; future marriage patterns in, 141

One-parent families, 21

Paul, St; teaching on marriage and divorce, 16, 17, 75

Peking man, 34

Penn, William, 86

Pennsylvania, 86

Perversion, sexual; 74; *see also* homosexuality, lesbianism

Place, Francis; essayist on contraception, 98

Pleistocene period, 34, 38

Polygamy; economic benefits of, 115; abolition in India, 125; Koran approval of, 126; Mormons' practice of, 134; in USA, 135; to increase birth rate, 135; future of, 136-7

Poor Law Acts, 83